Overtime
THE BONUS
Years

What happens when
you take the chance
to start your life over?

Ben E. Dickerson, Ph.D.
& Captain Ken Arthur

POWER PUBLISHING
Incorporated
Indianapolis, IN

Overtime: The Bonus Years

Ben Dickerson, Ph.D., and Captain Ken Arthur

ISBN-13: 978-0-9787268-4-3
ISBN-10: 0-9787268-4-7

Library of Congress Control Number: 2006932145

Power Publishing
5641 W. 73rd St.
Indianapolis, IN 46278
(317) 347-1051
www.powerpublishinginc.com

This book is manufactured in the United States of America.

Published by Power Publishing
5641 W. 73rd St.
Indianapolis, IN 46278

Editor: Janet Schwind
Cover Design: Parada Design

About the Authors

Ben Dickerson is a native Texan. Overtime: The Bonus Years is the culmination of his academic research into how individuals view their middle and later years. His careers include teaching and administrative assignments for several universities. Ben earned his undergraduate and master's degrees from Texas A & M University, and his Ph.D. from LSU (Baton Rouge). Ben and his wife, Florence, have seven children and sixteen grandchildren. The Dickersons reside in North Texas.

Ken Arthur is also a native Texan. He has been a minister, an Air Force fighter pilot, an airline captain, and is now in business management. He has an undergraduate degree in psychology and a master's degree in education. Ken is married to his high school sweetheart, Mary. They have a daughter, Kristi, and a son and daughter-in-law, Kevin and Celia. The Arthurs also live in Texas.

Dale —
When I grow up, I want
to be an instructor just like you!
Best wishes, My Friend —

Ken Arthur
JOSHUA 1:9
FEB '08

Dedications

From Ben, this book is dedicated:

To my wife Florence, whose skill as a physical therapist has made the bonus years of so many a time of wellness. Her drive is an encouragement and her caring spirit is an inspiration to everyone who knows her. Florence's devotion to me and our blended family can only come from God's eternal love. Her life is a testament of one who knows how to win in "overtime."

From Ken, this book is dedicated:

To my wife Mary – for making my *job* a joy;
To Kristi – for being the kind of daughter who makes her father proud;
To Kevin – for being the kind of man I wish I was;
To Celia – a daughter-in-law from Heaven;
To Terry – my hero, whose battle against cancer is an inspiration;
To Mom Campbell – for loving a son-in-law as a son;
To Mom – for living the bonus years with grace, love, and enthusiasm; and
To Granny, Aunt Jim, and Dad Campbell – *Requiescat in pace.*

From both Ben and Ken, this book is also dedicated to you, our readers, with the hope that your bonus years will be a time of joy, passion, adventure, peace, and newness of spirit every day. Go win the game!

Foreword

Really it's not easy to find something to occupy one's life after a career of driving open wheel race cars at over 200 miles per hour.

In 1994, I made the decision to leave competitive racing, but there were still things I wanted to accomplish. I agreed to be a consultant to the Indy Racing League (IRL) when it started in 1996.

Among my new career duties are driving the Pace Car before every IRL race and overseeing the rookies joining the Indy Racing League and the rookie orientation program for the Indianapolis 500. I've seen this as a way to give something back to the people and the sport that was so good to me and my family through the years.

Obviously, winning the Indianapolis 500 three times as well as two Indy Car Championships and being National Sprint Car Champion were great experiences and some of the highlights of my career. Now that I drive the Pace Car for the IRL races, it means I lead every lap I'm on the race track. More importantly, I'm still around people I enjoy and the sport I love. What better way to take advantage of my bonus years.

Overtime: The Bonus Years is full of stories from men and women who are winners. They've kept going when the odds were against them. They've found ways to reach their goals when things got tough. They haven't let problems or adversity crush them.

I hope their experiences will help you see something every race car driver knows: Sometimes winning comes to the individual who just refuses to give up.

Best wishes to you as you read this book.

—Johnny Rutherford

Introductions

Ben Dickerson and Ken Arthur have known each other for more than thirty years. Ben was initially Ken's professor at Stephen F. Austin State University in Nacogdoches, Texas. There was initially nothing to make them friends. One was a professor with a doctorate, the other an undergraduate student working on a bachelor's degree. The one drawing factor was that Ken and his wife Mary earned much needed money by babysitting the Dickersons' children.

After college graduation, Ken moved on to graduate school and his careers. Ben soon moved to become a professor at Baylor University in Waco, Texas. The Dickersons and Arthurs eventually lost track of each other.

Years passed and Ken's daughter was in Baylor, where she took a class from a professor named Dr. Ben Dickerson. Ken and Mary found this the perfect opportunity to see Ken's former mentor. More than two decades after Ken was in Ben's class and their lives had taken radically different directions, the two men have rediscovered some very strong ties from which a deep friendship has grown.

Both men have a deep faith, have been military officers, are pilots, enjoy the company of risk takers and entrepreneurs, see life as a gift to be savored, and are "life long learners." Likewise, both men have adult children who continue to be sources of great joy. Ben and Ken even discovered a common love for racquetball, which continues with occasional competitions even now.

Ben continues to challenge his former student by "assigning him" mandatory books to read. Ken responds by tutoring Ben with his ongoing computer skills education.

Together, they have a deep love and appreciation for helping others to reach their highest possible potential ... especially in their *Overtime, The Bonus Years.*

Enjoy!

Acknowledgments

No one ever writes a book and sees it published without the help of a large number of people. We want you to know about a few people who have been crucial to making us who we are today and who have made this book possible.

Tad Long is a publisher with a remarkable vision for his company, Power Publishing. Tad accepts, prints, and distributes books that uplift the spirit and quality of life of his readers. For us, he has been an encourager and mentor. Tad is a gentleman with the gift of drawing out the best from his authors.

Janet Schwind is the perfect editor. She took our diamond-in-the-rough manuscript and polished every facet until it was the brightest possible gem. Besides her skill as an editor, Janet has a sense of humor and contagious enthusiasm that make her a joy to work with.

The authors of each chapter have shared their lives in deeply personal and magnificent ways. We're grateful for their honesty, their dedication, and their amazing gift of touching others' lives.

From Ben: I want to recognize the faculty at Texas A&M and Louisiana State University who served as role models in how to "Make It Happen" in overtime. They did more than just provide information. Instead, they instilled a desire to reach the highest possible goals and to never quit trying. I'm proud to be a product of their training and encouragement.

Likewise, my pastor and mentor, Gordon Whitelock, impressed me with the importance of being spiritually healthy throughout the life course. His emphasis on studying the scriptures and the importance of praying each step of life's way has enabled me to experience an abundant life in the bonus years.

Ken Arthur is what everyone wishes for in a friend and colleague. His contributions to this book are priceless. He not only provided encouragement and meaningful discussion for me, but to every contributing author of this book. His exceptional intellect, drive, and focus kept all of us on the right track as well as ensuring our movement toward completing this project.

From Ken: It's been said that "good guys finish last." My best friend, David Marks, is proof that old adage is wrong. David is a successful entrepreneur, real estate developer, rancher, and sportsman. While success sometimes makes lesser men arrogant or self-centered, David's achievements have not changed him at all. His true humility, genuine caring spirit, and positive attitude have always been his defining characteristics. With David, the glass is always more than half full.

For almost two decades, David has been more like a brother than a friend. Dr. Wayne Dyer said it well: "A friend is a person with whom I may be sincere. Before him, I may think aloud." That describes David. He is always a tremendous encourager to me during both good times and bad. I wish every one of you could have a "David" in your lives ... the world would be a better place to live and everyone's bonus years would be a lot richer.

Through the years, Ben Dickerson has been a professor, a mentor, an advisor, and a coauthor. Best of all, he's always been a friend. Ben has a gift for making people around him feel exceptional. Plus, I suspect on his 100th birthday, Ben will draw me aside and say, "Ken, I've got this terrific book you need to read." And I'll read it. Blessings on you, Ben.

Contents

Foreword *v*

Introductions *vi*

Acknowledgments *vii*

1. **Overtime – The Bonus Years**
   Ben Dickerson Ph.D. and Captain Ken Arthur *1*

2. **Salt Water Up My Nose**
   Janet Schwind *13*

3. **Uncharted Waters**
   Mike Holt *27*

4. **Beyond Words – Reading Between the Lines**
   Mary Arthur, Ed.D. *37*

5. **Non Traditional – Who Says?**
   Don Andrews *47*

6. **Stepping Out In the Midst of Change**
   Stacey Condit Campbell *59*

7. **Spreading the Seeds of Opportunity**
   Mona Parish *75*

8. **Cleared For a Visual Approach**
   Ken Arthur *85*

9. **"With Your Next Husband"**
   Gay Bearden *97*

10. **Chase and Embrace Your Chazown!**
    Lance Robertson *107*

11. **Do You Know Where You Are Now?**
    Lou Stoops *119*

12. **Are You Ready For Your Overtime – The Bonus Years?**
    Ben Dickerson, Ph.D. and Captain Ken Arthur *131*

OVERTIME – THE BONUS YEARS
Ben Dickerson and Ken Arthur

It ain't over 'til it's over.
—Yogi Berra

The Game

It's a clear Saturday afternoon in the late fall. The air is crisp and cold, and the stadium is filled to capacity. The television audience includes millions more. This is the biggest game of the year with fans of both teams loudly cheering their players on.

For four quarters the home team has trailed on the scoreboard, but even with less than a minute in regulation play, no one is leaving their seats.

With ten seconds on the clock, the quarterback looks long and throws a deep sideline pass, hoping for either a touchdown or an interference penalty on the opposition. Neither happens. The ball is nearly intercepted then sails through the open arms of his favorite receiver.

The crowd screams its disapproval. The home team has no time-outs remaining and the coaches are desperate... It's fourth down and five yards to go. The score is 21 to 24 in favor of the visiting team. There are three seconds on the clock and the ball is on the 40 yard line.

What to do? The coaches on both sides know there isn't time for anything except a desperation field goal attempt. With a 50 yard kick as the only option, a nervous field goal kicker runs on the field.

His longest successful kick in seven seasons has been 46 yards.

Now with his team's entire season resting on this one play, he looks at the goal posts, which appear tiny in the distance. Half of the fans in the stadium become quiet while the other half yell louder in an attempt to distract the player. He feels the pressure of his whole career resting on the next three seconds.

Millions of eyes stare intently at the ball as the center approaches it. The player who will catch the snap and place it precisely for the kicker rubs the sweat from his hands. He feels the pressure, too.

The kicker carefully positions himself exactly in the right place to make this one play. He has practiced just such a kick hundreds of times. Now, if he misses, the entire team's season is finished. A good kick means the game will be tied and will go into overtime.

Once the ball is hiked into the air, everything goes into slow motion for the kicker. He sees the lace on the football as it spirals back. He watches the holder catch the ball and move it perfectly in place. The defense is crushing in to stop the play.

The kicker knows it's going to be good even before his foot hits the ball. His form is perfect, the ball placement is flawless, and the defense is a half-second late.

Time goes to zero on the scoreboard even while the ball is in the air. It's long enough, it's straight enough, and the referees on both sides of the goalpost raise their hands to signal a good kick. Everyone is amazed except the kicker.

The score is now 24 to 24 and the game goes into overtime.

Overtime. Now each team will send their captains back on the field to flip a coin to see who will receive the kick and continue the championship game. In this league, overtime is played as sudden-death, which means the first team to score any points wins the game and the championship trophy.

The home team wins the toss and chooses to receive the kickoff. The crowd is on its feet and chanting loudly as the overtime kickoff is made. Back on his eight yard line the receiver moves to catch the ball. His teammate quickly yells for him to make a "fair catch." This way he can't run, but the ball will be placed all the way to the 20 yard line.

Instead of heeding this advice, the receiver makes a running catch of the ball and tucks it firmly under his arm. He sees opposing jerseys in every direction, and chooses to run right up the middle of the field.

The stadium crowd grows louder; in millions of homes people are yelling at their television sets. The coaches and teammates are running along the sidelines, but the receiver is oblivious to everything except his desire to reach the goal line. Tackle after tackle is missed. Yard by yard the receiver breaks left and right until finally he breaks free, sprints the last 25 yards, and crosses into the end zone.

Even though they had trailed in the score for the entire regulation game, the home team won in overtime.

The Overtime of Life's Game – The Rules Are Changing

This story reflects the truth of our lives today. Overtime, in the game we described, provided a second chance for the home team to win. In our 21st century lives, we've been given "overtime" in our life expectancy. Overtime, that time mid-life when we thought the outcome was pretty much inevitable—but suddenly a whole new expanse of time is laid down before us like a precious, unexpected gift. A second chance to go for the win—and the possibilities again seem limitless.

Latest research by demographers and gerontologists indicates we have on average 30 "bonus years." These are the years when our parents and grandparents were finishing their lifetime careers and going into retirement. Today, with medical care prolonging our lives and individuals sometimes having four or five different careers, we see those same years differently than did those who raised us. For us, this additional third of life can be the best years to pursue opportunities, goals and dreams we have perhaps put off or figured we'd get to "someday."

Our increased longevity has produced some unexpected challenges. Historically, our culture has been somewhat blinded to overtime because of the way we view our life course such as birthdays, retirement, and life events. This linear way of seeing life is changing. Social norms are being altered by the actions and endeavors of the significant number of adults in their bonus years. For example:

- There are more students entering the arena of higher education later in life. Despite these greater numbers, they are still considered "non-traditional" students.
- People are now having more than one retirement. Multiple careers are becoming the norm. Just a generation ago people had one job their entire life. The career game has changed.
- People are getting married and having children later in life.
- There are far greater numbers of grandparents who are now raising their grandchildren.

Just as the football player in our story kicked better than he'd ever kicked in his whole life when he tied the game, we as individuals are in a similar situation. We're having to redefine our lives and our expectations of what we can accomplish.

In their book *Clicking*, futurist Faith Popcorn and her colleague Lys Marigold are among the first to recognize a trend that is contributing to a change in patterns of living for individuals in their 40s, 50s, 60s, and 70s. She refers to this trend as "down-aging." In other words, one's age is no longer the marker as to when one is eligible or ineligible to pursue their passions. People are ignoring their chronological age and redefining their social age. Even as we accept the fact that we are able to do more with our lives at a time when our parents were completely retired, we have to believe it possible. In our football example, even though the odds were against them, the kicker knew he could make his field goal and the receiver believed he could run for a touchdown. They had to put action to their acceptance in order to reach their goals.

To paraphrase the great Satchel Paige, how old would you be if you didn't know how old you are? In other words, if you didn't know your birth year, how old would you think you are? For most of us, we think as if we are several years younger than our chronological years.

The bonus years enable each of us to have greater flexibility to develop options and choices we can make. They provide unique avenues to come closer to living the passions of our lives.

What Others Have Said

We have found numerous books that address the way people look and grow in their later years. These authors have tackled many physical, sociological, psychological, and theological (spiritual) challenges faced by people entering years they didn't expect to see.

Zig Zigler in his book *Better Than Good* underscores the importance of passion, peak performance, and purpose as concepts that lead individuals to successful pathways. We have found Zig Zigler's insight to be crucial to winning in overtime.

Kenneth Cooper, M.D. in his book *Regaining the Power of Youth at Any Age* discusses the experiencing of symptoms that slow people down and interfere with peak performances at middle age and older. He speaks regarding wrong expectations about health and the aging process. Dr. Cooper examines exhaustion from technology and information overload, tension caused by time pressures, feelings of no longer competing at a high level, and many other causes of drain from our lives. He provides a methodology that is more than the typical fitness workout in resolving this all-too-common drain in our everyday lives.

Traveling Light, an inspirational book by Max Lucado, speaks about the excess baggage we sometimes carry such as fear, worry, and discontent. He suggests that this excess baggage wears us out. Using Psalm 23 from the Bible as our guide, he strongly suggests we rid ourselves of the added load to more fully enjoy the journey of life.

Another well-known author, Gene Cohen, M.D., Ph.D., has written a highly respected book, *The Creative Age*. As a psychiatrist, he provides a new perspective for looking beyond the stereotypes that overwhelm the majority of us as members of the baby boomer generation.

Bob Buford, author of *Half Time, Game Plan,* and *Finishing Well*, gives considerable attention to "what people who really live do differently." In the last book, Buford talks with 120 people he refers to as "code breakers." These people have deciphered what it takes to *finish well.*

Prime Time by Marc Freedman states, "… The boomers will not accept the old notions of later life in retirement…" He continues by saying, "Ultimately, our best hope is in a new vision—and a new practice of later life…"

Each of these books has contributed significantly to successful living for their readers. They have addressed the concerns and aspirations of a multitude of seekers.

Our Purpose

This book is designed for those readers who are not satisfied with the predictability of their lives. They find themselves in circumstances they wish to change. Thus, to win in the overtime or bonus years of their lives, they want to find the courage to act upon the visions they've always had … to accomplish what they never thought would happen … to know when their days are complete that there are no "I wish I had done this" dreams unfulfilled.

As the designers of this book, we have selected to share with you some exceptional individuals who have met the challenge of their bonus years and have created life-changing and exciting opportunities. While they are exceptional in their vision, they are no different than you are right now. They found new pathways to meet their goals and fulfill their dreams.

Just as professional coaches must devise new game plans to address each individual opponent, these authors have lived unique and innovative game plans to help them reach their goals.

The men and women you'll meet in this book have lived their lives with a "cyclical pattern of life" instead of a "linear" one.

Cyclical patterns make overtime a reality, because they happen to people who explore new avenues over several periods of their lives. People who have looked at their accomplishments and goals as starting points instead of destinations live in cyclical patterns. In contrast, a generation ago, many people lived linear lives where they had one career and followed the same pattern with little variation. They had the same job at the same company with the same work schedule without change. What that generation considered stable and secure, most of us today would find boring and repetitious. Linear patterns are not acceptable to those living vibrant overtime years.

The Cyclical Journeys of Ten Extraordinary People

The stories you are about to read are from 10 different authors. Each has a unique way of writing that the authors feel illustrates their individual experiences.

You'll notice quickly as you read this book that there is no "cookie-cutter" format. Some of the authors have added suggested reading while others quote favorite books. Some ask questions outright while others imply their questions. Each author has his or her own style of writing. As editors, we made a conscious decision not to change the flavor or uniqueness of each author by revising their style to make them sound the same.

Henry David Thoreau said, "Go confidently in the direction of your dreams. Live the life you've imagined." Ralph Waldo Emerson said, "Do not follow where the path may lead. Go instead where there is no path and leave a trail." Robert Frost spoke of the "road less traveled."

Each author has followed Thoreau's, Emerson's and Frost's encouragement. They've moved their lives down paths that were unanticipated and yet exciting.

They also have rejected the idea presented in Doris Day's beautiful song, *Whatever Will Be, Will Be (Que Sera, Sera)*. They didn't accept the logic that "what ever will be will be." Instead they created their own destiny.

As you read this book, you will meet some extraordinary people. It's our belief you may discover you are not so different from them.

Janet Schwind was a successful advertising copywriter when a series of life changing "waves" hit her. Within a short time, she had every major stabilizing structure in her life removed. Given the options of wallowing in self pity and despair or actively creating ways to mend her life, Janet chose to be proactive. Her way of meeting challenges and obstacles head-on will inspire you. Her infectious wit and humor will encourage you to face life with a positive attitude.

Mike Holt had a challenging childhood. His life easily could have been a tragedy. Instead you'll meet a man who faces challenges head on and finds a way to succeed. Mike and his wife Janet, with a very minimum of initial training and skill, decide to sail a 34-foot catamaran around the Gulf of Mexico. Their preparation, education, and experiences will make you laugh and excite you with the possibilities of fulfilling your own dreams without waiting for "one of these days."

Mary Arthur was the consummate wife and mother. She put her career as an educator on hold until her children were in school themselves, and only then did she return to the classroom. Later, she felt a desire to work on a master's degree. While still a full-time teacher, she finished her first advanced degree. The opportunity to continue on with a doctorate was a distant possibility until the university she attended enticed her with a fellowship. She discovered it's never too late to go back and start or complete an education at any level. Dr. Mary Arthur will encourage your desire to work, sacrifice, and reach your potential regardless of your age.

Don Andrews was a high school and semi-pro hockey player. His career led him into sports medicine where he saw an untapped potential. By building a company that has provided sports medicine personnel for such organizations as NASCAR, American Le Mans Series (ALMS), Professional Bull Riders (PBR), Championship Bull Riders (CBR), Champ Car World Series (CCWS), Professional Rodeo Cowboys Association (PRCA), and the US Pro Ski Tour, Don has blazed a trail. His example of "thinking outside the box" and discovering a need he could answer will inspire you to look for opportunities you can meet regardless of where you are right now.

Stacey Campbell is a wife and a mother of three wonderful and energetic girls. She's learned that change in life is an integral part of the journey. She recognizes that some change is normal; other times it's thrown at you without warning, and occasionally change is self-inflicted. Stacey's grown to believe the real test of a successful life is how gracefully and joyfully one accepts change and uses it to further personal, intellectual, and spiritual growth. Stacey says, "My story is like so many—one filled with joys, sorrows, hopes, fears, and love. Life is truly a roller coaster (and I am no fan of those)! So for me, learning to accept and even embrace the ups and downs, and to make them work for me, has been the challenge." You'll be inspired by Stacey's story and her amazing response to change.

For Mona Parish, a path that began with a desire to find a constructive way to help women facing unplanned or crisis pregnancies has led to a full-time executive ministry position. Appalled by abortion protesters who offered insults and condemnation, yet no practical solutions or assistance for women outside a women's clinic in her hometown of Houston, Texas, Mona began volunteering at a crisis pregnancy center four hours a week. That four hour weekly commitment grew into a temporary job, and from there into a permanent staff position. Mona now serves as executive director of the center where she began as a volunteer. Her story will illustrate how saying "yes" to small steps in your life can bring you to a new level of service and commitment.

Ken Arthur grew up believing his direction in life was set. He was going to be a minister. After finishing his seminary training and becoming a college minister, he recognized this was not his true calling. Instead, Ken followed his real dream and became an Air Force fighter pilot. After almost a decade in the military, Ken became a commercial pilot, ending his career as a captain for a major airline. Even after this third career, he chose to start a fourth career in business. Ken wants you to realize that regardless of how far you've come, it's never too late to change directions in your life.

Gay Bearden is a high school teacher with a talent for influencing the lives of her students. In two and a half decades in the classroom, she has taught students to consider the more profound aspects of lifelong citizenship. In her government and law studies classes, she emphasized the right of "life, liberty, and the pursuit of happiness" to her students. Her life took a major shift when her husband passed away. Suddenly, Gay was compelled to rediscover herself as more than a wife, mother, and teacher. This dynamic woman's experience of moving beyond widowhood will be an inspiration to everyone who has faced tragedy and not only survived, but grown.

Lance Robertson is a man whose life was filled with considerable activity. His life was totally consumed with the university where he worked. After many years, Lance came to realize the importance of having more in life. He discovered a Hebrew word, "chazown," which means "vision." Lance encourages his readers to chase their own chazown.

Lou Stoops is a man who was blessed to have an extraordinary mother. When he was a boy, she had a great way of teaching him how to navigate around their city. She would ask him, "Do you know where you are now?" By doing this, she encouraged him to always recognize the importance of observing the many landmarks and signposts needed to guide him to a destination. Lou has realized that there have been landmarks and signposts in his life as he's navigated through career transitions. Even with his "navigation skills," like most of us, Lou has also encountered some personal detours and "dead ends" along the journey. His story will inspire and encourage you as you navigate your life, too.

Your Role In This Book

As you read each chapter, try to put yourself in the place of the author. Think of their stories as game films to prepare you for an overtime game. Use their experiences to help you create a game plan for your own life. All coaches, regardless of the sport, recognize the need for flexibility in their game plans. Unexpected events on the field require them to make changes.

Flexibility and preparation have always been crucial to success. There is a classic football story known to every Texas A&M Aggie. In 1922, Dana X. Bible, the Texas A&M football coach, had a minimum of players for his team. A hard first half of the game had left A&M with too few players to play the remaining half. Fortunately, there was a man in the stands named King Gill who, while not an actual member of the team, had still practiced and learned the team's plays. He was smaller than most players and an unlikely football hero. Instead of giving up in the face of almost certain defeat, Coach Bible called this "player" from the stands. According to Aggie history, King Gill quickly suited up, came on the field and miraculously helped win the game. That was the beginning of the A&M tradition of the "Twelfth Man." To this day, every Aggie stands up continuously throughout every football game. By standing, they are each symbolically there to do whatever is needed for victory.

Just as Coach Bible was flexible enough to call upon a student from the stands to help his team, we hope you will call upon the authors of each chapter. Although none of our authors have faced the same challenges you face or walked the same path as you, it is our hope that, by reading of their pilgrimages, you will draw inspiration to drive for a touchdown in the overtime years of your life.

In any football game that enters overtime, there is a special excitement. It's a second chance to win. The team that wins is usually the one that draws on an inner strength or a deeper desire to finish first.

Your overtime or bonus years can easily be the most exciting ones you live.

Enjoy!

Ben and Ken

Chapter 2

SALT WATER UP MY NOSE
Janet Schwind

I wish I could pull off the surfer thing. I would be so cool, with my scrunchety, belligerent beach hair and puka shell necklace and gritty tan. I would hang out at the beach café sipping lemonade and shining my surfboard and telling people really awesome stories of how, like, I caught the big wave. But, this probably will never happen because, a) I'm afraid of man-eating sharks, and b) I'm oceanically challenged in Indiana.

The thing about major life changes is that they often come in waves, so just as you're gulping for air after the first one hits, another one is smacking you upside the head and slamming salt water up your nose.

My first wave was a doozy. It hit in July 2003 when my husband checked out of our eight-year marriage. It came as a bit of a surprise—and not the happy kind where I receive gifts of jewelry or chocolates. We went to church together, everyone liked us, and there had been no bad weather reports leading up to this. I'm thinking, wait a second, this can't be happening. I'm a *Christian,* for pete's sake! As a major life change, broken marriage = not good. As a rapid weight loss plan, very good.

Although my pants were fitting me much better, the reality of aloneness wasn't. For a wave this big, I turned to my church, family and friends for support. I didn't have the energy—or maybe the confidence—to handle it myself. It seemed like a good time to get closer to God. I had some questions for him.

My good friend Amy Knauer took me in during the weeks immediately following the split. It was a good place to be. I was able to take some time off work and just be sad. I sat on the deck in Amy's backyard with my Bible reading Psalms a lot. I'd weep and then read and then weepily read and then take a break for snacks and weep some more. The copious crying thing lasted only about a week. During this time I was able to ask God all the whys, and just release my hurt to him from the wretched depths. Have you ever had a time that was very sad but very good at the same time? This was one of those times. I let it all out. It was like God was hanging out with me beneath the trees, putting his arm around my shoulder, comforting me and supplying me with tissues.

As the months passed, I worked through various stages of anger, denial and finally acceptance. During my anger stage, all I could think about was how I somehow got stuck in the exact role I vowed I would never be in: divorced at 40. How cliché. I was everything I never hoped to be. I was the star of a bad sitcom. "Suddenly Single. An extraordinarily fashionable, very youthful looking woman suddenly finds herself starting over mid life." I didn't ask for this; why wasn't I given a chance to repair things? Months later another horrifying thought arose: I have to date again. *That* made me mad. My first overtime episode didn't feel so much like a bonus.

Time, good friends, God and comfort food work miracles. As I worked through things, I found a resiliency I didn't expect. I didn't feel as if my world had crumbled. I was a lot different than when I had faced adversity in the past. I had a foundation. I really felt God's presence keeping me grounded and feeding me with the knowledge of who I am in him. Jesus' words stayed in my mind all the time: "Never will I leave you; never will I forsake you."

Despite the occasional sad memories—not to mention a whirlwind of other high-stress events around this time, including a bankruptcy and a trusted friend who'd hurt us—I was mending. I forgave my wayward spouse after a few months. I was closing a door.

Once you forgive, however, things don't always spring back to normal like the Pillsbury Doughboy's belly. I was still having bad dreams, in which my worst fears came true just like in my real life. I would sometimes wake up with this heavy sadness and realize I needed to pull myself out of it again because this alone thing was now my "new normal."

Apparently I still had some healing to do. I asked God to do that for me. I have always read books and articles on relationships and psychology, and I knew that forgiving was the first step, but that healing still needed to take place. I knew that the measuring stick for healing would be when I could think back over the memories without any pain. It would be like indifferently reviewing the tapes of someone else's life. Eventually I realized one day that I was there. The bad dreams had stopped and I was no longer feeling hurt. I was even getting my joy back. God had been faithful once again in his promise to me: "He heals the brokenhearted and binds up their wounds." (Psalm 147:3)

Wave one had been formidable and really messed up my hair, but I rode it out. Wave two was self induced and hit a couple years later.

I should mention now that my 20-some professional working years had been spent as an advertising copywriter—if you want to call that writing. You know those people you see in the movies who come up with the inane ads and jingles, the people whose offices are stocked with rubber chickens, squirt guns and other assorted toys. That was me.

It had been a good career for the most part. Creative, fun, always something new. And the people you meet in advertising, well, they're what I like to call "a little bit of crazy." I started my career out of college as an editor and quickly moved into the copywriting niche, where I stayed for the next two decades. My pay had steadily increased and, by the last job, I was making more money than I had ever imagined a goofball like me could make.

And yet, for the past several years, a growing discontent had begun to nibble at me like a cute little bunny rabbit with big pointy teeth. I'd been battling the feeling that advertising just didn't have any meaning for me anymore. Actually I don't think it *ever* had any meaning for me. While my colleagues marveled at the incredibly imaginative ways to sell deodorant, I rolled my eyes thinking to myself, "Uh, they're stupid TV commercials." Perhaps I never had the proper passion for the job. It paid the bills, though, and—except for the unpaid overtime hours, the never getting credit for my work and clients constantly rewriting my words—it was a great job.

But there I was in January of 2005, in a flurry of emotion and other confusing vibes, running screaming from my job. This particular job I'd been at almost ten years, so I was leaving some stability. But, I just burned out. I couldn't write one more stupid brochure for some company I didn't care about. The emotions were really more complex than that; somehow the divorce had played a part in my state of turmoil, but I still can't precisely explain all of what I was feeling that precipitated this career crisis.

I accepted a job offer from another advertising agency, and I quit my job to start this new one, thinking the change of scenery would do the trick. I quickly realized it wouldn't. Two weeks later, in what was starting to look like a bad habit, I was ready to quit my job, again, amid a second flurry of tears (this would NOT look good on a resume).

Again guess who was the lucky recipient of my problems? Amy! I told her that I just didn't think I could muster the inspiration to write ad copy anymore. Actually it felt impossible at that point. It still hadn't dawned on me that I could do something permanent about it.

Amy said, "Quit."

"What?"

"Why don't you quit your job?"

"I can't just quit…can I?" But even as I was saying those words, the possibility of this option was taking root in my soul and filling me with a new sense of hope and freedom. I stopped weeping so I could eat an oatmeal cream pie and think. "But how would I live? I don't have any savings ... Wait, I do have some profit sharing…"

"Use it." (I love Amy, spending my retirement savings like that.)

"Well, I guess I could use that till I find another job." By this time my mind was all over the idea of quitting—hugging and kissing and caressing the idea, in fact. The next day I called my employer and asked to meet with him. We met at the local coffee shop, and through tears (I promise I am really not a hugely weepy person), I said I needed to quit, not just the job but this career. My employer, a very cool Christian guy, was extremely supportive of my decision. It felt good to have his backing. Although I had only been there a few weeks I really saw integrity and character in these people and I was sad to be leaving them and disappointing them at the same time.

So now I was unemployed! And I didn't qualify for unemployment. Oops. Had I made a grievous mistake? I never felt any regrets about the decision. (Except the fact that I had quit during the wintertime and couldn't go outside and play.) The first few months I let myself rest. I burned several weeks watching the first three seasons of *Alias* on DVD. Then I borrowed Amy's *Friends* collection on DVD, five seasons.

Again, I realized I had some healing to do. My writing career had very literally sucked the life out of me creatively. I felt beaten up and useless as a writer. I felt I had nothing to offer. I turned my back on anything creative. My old hobbies of jewelry making and drawing held no joy for me. I couldn't muster it anymore.

This leaving my career thing was a whole new deal. I had always defined myself by my job. I'm a copywriter. I write ads. That's what I do. So if I wasn't a copywriter anymore, what was I? I had plenty of spare time to ponder this at the local coffee shop.

I thought about my life and what I would do with it. This was a hugely foggy topic for me. I didn't have another "dream job" in mind…copywriting *was* my dream job. In fact I didn't feel like I was qualified to do anything. My thoughts progressed into darker and darker places. "I am not good at anything. There is no job out there for me. I will never work again. I'll live on the streets. I can do some lovely things with cardboard." I think Satan was pulling out the stops to push me down into hopelessness. I had to combat the negative thoughts that snuck in; most days I did well, others not so good. My future was lying there in front of me like a gift, but I was feeling too unsure to open it. And that's weird because anyone who knows me knows I love presents.

As friends and family began to hear about me quitting my job, I started getting their unsolicited feedback. Most of it was positive and supportive. I can't tell you how many people said, "I wish I could do that" or "That's really brave, it takes a lot of faith." To be honest, I didn't feel brave or faithful—I thought I might be somewhat retarded like my brothers told me when I was little.

Some people didn't understand. "You don't even have a plan." It miffed me a little to hear this. Life is messy sometimes. No, I don't have everything planned out. Actually the idea of a wide-open future was starting to feel exhilarating. It had adventure written all over it. This wave, my second overtime, began to feel like a windfall—the chance to start my life over.

Spring, however, had come and I developed a fondness for the leisurely life of the unemployed. I enthusiastically embraced the ways of the Day Dwellers who I'd always envied—those people who are out enjoying the sunshine while the rest of the unfortunate masses are huddled in their little cubicles, their eyelids having evolved to thin membranes sufficient to screen out weak fluorescent lighting. I liked what I had become…a coffeehouse slacker! Life felt real again. I was out in the world roaming free instead of chained to a desk. I began to walk upright; the oppression of decades of working for "the man" had been lifted.

I tried some of the suggestions well-meaning friends offered. *What Color Is Your Parachute?*, an outstanding book for helping individuals decide on career choices, was, for me, just a little too fundamental. I already had my colors picked out. I tried going through one of those workbooks that hones in on your character traits to help you write your own mission statement, and thus focus on finding a new career. One of the exercises had me writing things in my journal like:

Janet is like the wind.
Janet is a tree.

Janet is wasting journal paper.

Most of the workbook questions I just didn't know the answers to. I made my dear friend Ryan Fuller, bless his heart, fill out surveys about me because I felt so unclear about what I wanted to do. All of the job suggestions given me by my friends were starting to get on my little unemployed nerves. They were throwing things at me that I could not possibly enjoy or be good at. Restaurant manager. Insurance sales. Hello! I am creative. Are you *trying* to kill me? I was willing to take "just a job" to provide an income, but deep inside I knew that this was my time to make a leap and hold out for something more.

In my really-reaching-for-ideas stage, I looked into being a funeral director. I thought, I am a caring person; I could help people grieve *and* use my creative skills to design nice looking funerals. However, my skill set did not include the required draining of bodily fluids. Then I thought it would be a fun experiment to go to a hospital and apply for a job I'm ridiculously unqualified for.

"Hi, I'm applying for the brain surgeon position."

"What are your credentials?"

"I wrote a hospital brochure."

@!*@#%!! (Sounds of me being kicked to the curb.)

I test-drove a few jobs I thought might be my passions. One was working at a dog hotel. The pooches loved me, especially when I delivered their happy hour muttinis. I got peed on a few times but I just laughed it off as I washed it off. After a few months though this was getting old. Don't get me wrong—I loved making just above minimum wage, but I knew this wasn't going to sustain me in the lifestyle to which I had hoped to become accustom.

By this time, I realized I needed to find a real job so I could pay my bills and go to Starbucks whenever I wanted. I prayed, and here is what I asked God: "Please bring a job to me that is something I will enjoy and something I will be good at." A simple and direct request. I figured I'd take him up on that "ask and you shall receive" thing.

I chose this not-seriously-employed time in my life to try

something else I had always wanted to do: a mission trip. It was way out of my comfort zone to go to a foreign country with total strangers and sleep in bunk beds with lizards on the wall six inches from my face. I chose a trip to Nicaragua through an organization called Forward Edge International. It was probably the best thing I have ever done.

I felt like God gave me a huge glimpse into how big he really is and how he is already working all around us. I saw how easy it was to love people, even people who didn't speak my language. I learned how to say "girl blowing bubbles" in Spanish.

Upon my triumphant return, I forged ahead, applying for jobs I knew I wouldn't get but still knowing inside that God would bring the right job to me. It was hard to explain this to people, that God was going to get me a job. By this time I had come to the end of what I considered my available pool of funds, so I vacated my groovy bachelorette pad and humbly asked to move in with my little brother Dave, his wife Jodi and their two kids, Robbie and Annie. I hated the idea of having to barge in on my family but I was running out of cash and the sidewalk was looking very uninviting.

So there I was. Forty-two years old, living with my brother, and unemployed. I know, you want to date me.

Living with bro brought unexpected blessings. I enjoyed my friendship with Jodi as we spent more time with each other than ever. Dave's antics always kept things lively and fun. It was great to reconnect with the kids too. Annie made me a paper mailbox and set it outside my bedroom door and then started leaving me sweet little notes. I was there for both of the kids' first communions. I had grown up Catholic so I knew what a special day that was.

Little bro had given me a deadline of a couple months for moving out, and I was nearing the deadline but hadn't found a permanent job. By now it was December 2005 and I was temping with the state in the Office of Code Revision, proofing all the bills and amendments going through the legislature. It was a stress free, easy and flexible job that would prove again to be God's perfect provision to help me get through what was coming.

Wave three snuck up on me. I was at my annual breast exam, and the doctor said she discovered a tiny lump. I jokingly said, "That's my breast." But she insisted on an ultrasound. From the looks of things, she said, the lump didn't have the characteristics of cancer, and in the past I'd had fibrocystic lumps a plenty from massive coffee consumption, so neither of us was worried.

Then I got the phone call. "Turns out it is cancer after all."

"Really? Oh, crap."

My dad died of lung cancer in 1985 and there was plenty of other cancer on both sides of my family. But things like major diseases don't scare me; losing my debit card—now that scares me. Honestly, there was only one moment when I felt fear wash through me: In my initial meeting with the cancer surgeon, she laid out my treatment options and when she said that many women in my situation opt for a double mastectomy, I sort of freaked out. I have peace with larger issues like dying, but to live with parts of my body missing was something that terrified me. Did I really have to go such a radical route? As she spoke, the panic began to fade as I realized there was another option that seemed right for me. I went with the lumpectomy, and then skated through my 16 radiation treatments. I was fortunate that the type of cancer I had did not require chemotherapy; I did not want to lose this gnarly hair of mine. The cancer had not spread to the lymph nodes either, which was a bonus. My only side effects were a couple of weeks of severe migraines; my radiation program was a newer, shorter yet more intense treatment. I was just glad to have it over with so quickly and to start feeling better.

I was breezing through this cancer thing! I met plenty of people at the cancer center who were much worse off than I was. I felt guilty having people offering me support and sympathy. That's why I played my cancer card sparingly, using it only in rare instances like with my family, "Can I have that last potato? Come on, I have cancer."

People came out of the woodwork to encourage me. I got cards and emails and offers to help from my friends at church and my family. It was pretty awesome to feel so cared for. But what I didn't expect was how alone I felt.

How could I feel alone with all this support? It's hard to explain but I think that, no matter how many people were there to help, it was still just me with cancer and knowing I was the one who had to deal with it made me feel this unpleasant aloneness. I think I started praying more often around this time, and God was on it.

A new friend appeared on the scene. Jen Robinson and I connected at a community volunteer event through our church. The humor thing kicked in for both of us and this girl just made me laugh so much. She was frighteningly like me; I like that in a person. But much more than that she truly became a good friend who was there for me constantly through the cancer thing and beyond. I didn't feel so alone anymore.

Sometime or another during the summer of 2005 a random, lovely thought popped into my head. I felt that I would perhaps be offered a job through a friend and I would be working with a whole bunch of different people. It kind of felt like a "psychic" flash, like the time I correctly predicted Eddie Cheever would win the Indianapolis 500 (although not early enough to place a bet on him). But then I thought it was just my thought—or so I thought.

A few months later I attended a Vineyard church conference in Ohio. At one point they invited us up for prayer. I figured since I was still searching for my future, I could use all the prayers I could get. That's when a very nice lady, a total stranger, prayed for me, and told me that God said I would get a job through a friend and I'd be working with a bunch of different people. Hello! It was the precise wording as my "psychic" thought. This was the first time in my life I had confirmation that God actually spoke to me! I was pretty excited about it. I started feeling like, yes, maybe God wants to talk to ME, not just to the spiritually mature people who pray really eloquently. I felt sure God was going to take care of me, and I wasn't worried. Now I just had to be patient for his timing.

If you think it's exciting that I heard directly from the creator of the universe, how do you think I felt when his words came true? In April 2006 I got offered a job through my friend Kathy Malone at a publishing company working with lots of different people, like editors, authors, graphic designers and printers. Hey, that sounds like something God said to me once! I knew this was the job I'd prayed about.

Things weren't peachy at the beginning though. Even though I believed God had led me to this job, that jerk Satan was trying to steal my joy. I had a rough entry to the new job. Publishing was new to me; I felt overwhelmed and had this giant fearball (just like a furball, only you can't hack it up) ruining everything. It was that irrational kind of fear that paralyzes your brain so that you are non-functional. I kept thinking, why would God put me in this job; I hate it. But something deep down inside told me this WAS the job he picked for me and that somehow this was going to turn out alright.

It took me a few months and some antacids to work through this fear thing. I kept begging God to cure me of my fear, to just take it away. But one day I realized I was treating him like this Insty Cure God, demanding he magically fix me. I realized that was a lame way to treat God. I understood that maybe it was more of a partnership with me and him, that I needed to treat him like he has feelings, and talk to him every day and not just when I was demanding help. My relationship with God started changing.

A few months into the job, my fearball disintegrated. The owner of the company Al Long (we call him Doc) helped me realize I was in a safe place to learn and make mistakes. I grasped that it was okay for me not to know everything. He affirmed that God had indeed brought me there, and that they felt blessed to have me! This was quite a revolutionary concept.

This probably sounds cheesy, but I love my job now! I am doing all these things that I love, like reading manuscripts, editing, helping people write titles and subtitles for their books, and working with artists, and I feel somewhat competent again! What a great feeling.

And I work with this freakishly awesome family: Mom, Dad, Tad, Chad, and Brad. Those are their real names. They actually operate with integrity in everything they do. And they are really funny, all of them—I mean, their humor is exactly the same as mine. I feel joyful being there and I feel loved by them. And for the first time in decades I feel a blossoming passion for what I am doing. (That is actually miraculous.) Doc started the company because he felt God calling him to publish inspiring stories that would make a difference in people's lives. That's really what they care about. I actually see them carrying out this mission. It's not just some corporate policy written for an employee manual. Heck, we don't even have an employee manual.

I've been excited lately. About my job. About my brand new bachelorette pad. About being able to hear God. About talking with him more, and seeing more of his beauty. About this adventure that is my life. And when the next wave hits, I think I'll just get on top and ride it.

Five Thoughts on Riding Out the Waves of Change

1.   You are not your job. That's comforting because I used to make whoppers at Burger King. Find out who you are. What do you value? What are you passionate about? What noble things do you dream about? Become your true self.

2.   Jobs or other people can't be your security. That's a lot of responsibility to put on a person or a thing. Try God; he's faithful and he never changes.

3.   Life is messy. Don't expect things to go as planned or you'll be disappointed. Leave room for new possibilities to unfold. Like my dad always used to say, "A little dirt never hurt anybody."

4.   Listen for God. Learn to trust that inner voice; you're most likely not schizo. It's God whispering to you. Go ahead and trust it. It feels so good when you do. The more you trust it, the more you start to recognize the sound of his voice. It's pretty exciting stuff.

5.   God's always preparing you for what's to come. Although I couldn't see it then, now looking back it's so obvious that I was learning skills on my old job that would be the perfect experience for my new career. God is not going to throw you out there without a plan.

Know there will be times in your life when you get slammed

by wave after wave. You may be blowing salt water out your nose, but there's always the promise of better times ahead. When you're getting drenched, just straighten your puka shells, fix your eyes on the shore and swim like crazy for solid ground. Don't let anyone or anything take you down. Your most valuable gear to help you withstand life's waves is already inside you.

A Closing Thought From Ben and Ken

Abraham Lincoln said it well, "Most people are about as happy as they make up their minds to be." Janet reminds us of times in everyone's life when we get overwhelmed. Trouble and tragedy sometimes come in waves too fast to let you catch your breath and recover. Despite that, living our bonus years with gusto comes from realizing faith, perseverance, and a great sense of humor are balms to bring healing when life seems too hard to face. In short, you make up your mind to be happy and conquer the fear, the sadness, the difficulty.

Don't give up. Reread the five items that close Janet's chapter and really think about how those truths could encourage you wherever you are in your life's journey today.

UNCHARTED WATERS
Mike Holt

Grow old along with me! The best is yet to be.
—Robert Browning

Introduction

How many times have you said, "I'm going to do that one of these days"? "But," you tell yourself, "I'll have plenty of time for that later." Somehow there's always a reason (a.k.a. "excuse") to avoid leaving your comfort zone, to take a risk. I know. I thought the same way until one hot summer afternoon in 2003 when I had one of the strangest experiences of my life. That day, everything changed for me.

I'd spent the day playing softball and golf in a type of heat that can only be appreciated by those who've spent a summer in sultry Houston. After the last game, I didn't feel well and noticed that my thoughts were not as clear as they should have been. The next thing I remember is coming to my senses in the hospital that night about 11:00 p.m. I have no memories of the hours in between. My wife Janet tells me that when she had arrived home, I was confused and kept asking the same questions over and over. Fearing I'd had a stroke, she took me to the hospital emergency room.

They performed a multitude of tests, none of which I remember, but everything in my brain appeared normal. She also tells me I had a high old time joking with the nurses and left the doctors scratching their heads. The neurologists finally concluded I'd experienced "transient global amnesia." This strange disorder is reported in about 23 per 100,000 people each year and has sort of a Swiss cheese effect on the brain. Patients exhibit a dramatic loss of memory for recent events and cannot retain new information, but long-term memories are usually preserved. For example, I could remember my Social Security number, my birth date and my phone number, but not where I'd been yesterday. I remembered the names of friends, but not the trip we'd taken with them a few months before. I didn't know what year it was, much less the month or day, nor could I recall the name of the president. The cause of this unusual phenomenon is unknown, but the doctors think extreme physical stress can be a factor as can weightlifting or even sexual activity. Thankfully, it has no residual long-term effects, but it sure got my attention. "What if it *had* been a stroke?" is the question I kept asking myself. What if it had been the end? I decided "one of these days" had come.

Background

I think I was so resistant to change because of all the upheaval I had experienced in my early years. My parents were divorced when I was an infant. My mother was young, uneducated and not able to provide for me, so I lived with various relatives and saw her only occasionally. I barely remember my biological father. He came to visit only a few times and was killed in an accident when I was still a small child. When I was eight years old, my mother remarried and returned for me. I was terrified at the thought of being uprooted and moved to a new city. I recall sitting in the hall outside the courtroom during the custody hearing, thinking my world had come to an end. I most emphatically did not want to move, and I still remember some of my thoughts. "I'll never be able to watch Howdy Doody again," and "Who are these people?" I barely knew Mom and didn't know my new stepfather at all. It was an extremely stressful time in my young life.

After I moved to Houston, I happily discovered that Howdy Doody moved with me and, in time, I grew to love both my parents. My stepfather eventually became "Dad" and was a stabilizing force for me. He was a loving, patient man and my best fan. I still miss him. He died from heart disease with so many unrealized dreams when he was only 59 years old. I should have learned my lesson about the evanescence of life then, but it took my own experience 18 years later to drive the point home.

Comfortably ensconced in my new life, I saw no reason to rock my boat and resisted changes. I became quite a competent athlete, which was a good thing as we had very little money and it was my ticket to a higher education. Predictably, I chose a baseball scholarship at a junior college close to home over one at a major university out of state. I couldn't make myself leave my comfort zone. After graduation, I passed up a great coaching job at a college in another city for the same reason. That was the pattern of my life; find something comfortable, stay with it as long as I could with as few changes in the status quo as possible. In contrast, Janet is very much a "doer." She constantly urged me to get involved with new things and to make commitments for leadership roles — but I refused. My fear of failure was just too strong and anxiety-provoking. I agonized because my desire to live up to her expectations was overridden by my ever-present doubts. Everything changed that summer day.

Changes I Made In My Life

After what I've come to call my "episode," I found myself slowing down, paying more attention. I was surprised to realize that so much of what I'd always thought was important really wasn't; so much of what I worried about never came to pass. What a waste of precious time it is to focus on things that may not happen! I made the conscious decision to keep my thoughts in the present and was delighted to discover that the lifelong feelings of anxiety began to melt away. Janet remarked that I seemed to have more patience and was noticeably nicer to people. I knew that was because I was paying attention to them, actually listening rather than racing ahead to the next thought or the next activity. I was enjoying my newfound freedom so much I decided to venture a step further into uncharted territory.

We live on the Texas coast very near a lake that connects to

Galveston Bay. At the time of my epiphany we owned a small sailboat, but had only ventured out of the lake twice before. Although we'd taken sailing courses and I felt competent to handle the boat, the thought of taking it into the bay caused my constant companion, Anxiety, to leap into overdrive. Janet lives for adventure and loves the water. I knew she dreamed of buying a larger boat and taking it for a long cruise, and although we talked about it, I was never really serious. I thought it was one of those crazy ideas that would eventually go away. Now I asked myself, Why not? followed by Why not now? I allowed my new way of thinking to override my normal qualms and heard myself saying, "Let's buy a boat and take our trip." Surprised and pleased, Janet readily agreed.

It didn't take us long to find our perfect boat, a 34-foot sailing catamaran named Sea Level. She was located in Florida, which we saw as an opportunity to jump right in and get our feet wet (although not literally, we hoped) sailing her to Texas. With just the slightest bit of trepidation, we loaded a one-way rental van with provisions and headed east to bring our new boat home. This was quite a step for a guy who'd only ventured into the ocean, a bay actually, twice before. I hardly recognized my new self, but it was a heady feeling. I'll never forget the way I felt the day we threw off the lines and sailed away from Ft. Lauderdale. Was I scared? More like terrified, but also excited. I shelved all the What if? thoughts that tried to be heard and threw off my chains, too.

I wish I could tell you everything went perfectly on that trip, but I'd be lying. We ran aground (only once, but it was a humdinger), endured storms, lost our auto helm, and our steering wheel fell completely apart late one night. We discovered that our fuel gauges were faulty *after* a midnight, hair-raising sail to a fuel dock through the shallowest channel I've ever seen. Why do these things always happen in the wee hours?

But we got ungrounded, found shelter from the storm, used our sailing skills instead of the auto helm and repaired the steering wheel with a kitchen knife. We had many more good times than bad and, relieved and pleased, I managed to bring our boat safely into our slip in Houston. I learned a lot on that maiden voyage and my confidence grew.

Back in Texas, we took more classes to prepare for our cruise. While I learned diesel engine maintenance and electrical systems, Janet took courses in navigation. After more education and a lot of sailing up and down the Texas coast, we were ready. We prepared our house for an extended absence, arranged household help for my 81-year-old mother and on a cold day in February 2005, set sail from Houston. We planned to be tucked into a safe port by the start of hurricane season in June, but other than that, had no definite itinerary. That first hour I found myself accompanied by my old companion, Anxiety, asking, "Will you be able to handle all the situations that will inevitably occur? What if you aren't able to live up to Janet's expectations of you?" I also had some concerns about our relationship. We've always had a strong marriage, but how would being alone in such a confined space for months impact our relationship? Would it damage it? Improve it? I suppressed the thoughts by reminding myself that I was competent and resourceful and concentrated on the present. Let whatever happens happen. I relaxed. It felt good.

The Gulf Coast was littered with reminders of previous hurricanes. We saw houses along the shore line stripped naked to their studs, debris still littering the ground around them. Sailboats remained lodged in the tree line where they had been blown, and half-submerged barges created a new set of navigation hazards. A marina in Alabama where we'd bought fuel on our maiden voyage was all but destroyed. The top third of a sailboat mast protruded from brown, murky water where the end of a dock had been. I felt insignificant in the evidence of such power, and I doubled my resolve to be in our hurricane hole by June 1.

Florida waters are beautiful. We knew we'd arrived without even consulting a chart because of the abrupt change in water color from coffee brown to emerald green. We took our time, chose our weather carefully and hop-scotched our way down the west Florida coast. What a rare and wonderful thing it is to have no agenda! We stayed in ports until we were ready to move on, some much longer than others. The fabulous Greek food in Tarpon Springs kept us in port for almost two weeks. Our neighbors there were David and Sandy from Canada and Paul and Mary from New Jersey, all experienced sailors. I learned quite a bit from them about repairs and maintenance of Sea Level, and we enjoyed many nights of food, wine and camaraderie. We would continue to cross paths for the remainder of our journey. One of the greatest pleasures of the cruising lifestyle is making new friendships like these.

We also loved Ft. Myers Beach, where we moored for eight days, enjoying excellent live music and charity crab races at the marina's funky bar. We were there so often, the owners asked us to pose for a photo shoot for their website. As we entered the mooring field, we were hailed on the radio by Ron and Karla, new friends we'd met in Carrabelle. They were having lunch in a restaurant atop the bridge and saw our arrival. We spent several evenings swapping stories with them before their departure. We also met some nice folks who had just come from the Keys and they provided us with lots of useful information for our next leg.

Moving south, we left cities behind and entered the Everglades where we spent solitary nights anchored in coves among the mangroves. Night skies were brilliant with stars and the silence was broken only by the sounds of wildlife. In late April, we sailed into the crystal waters of the Florida Keys, first stop Key West. With the wind and waves behind us, we were doing a little over eight knots. That's a snail's pace on land, but on a sailboat, that's screaming. The Key West harbor is an extremely busy place and I had a few tense moments finding my way around a mammoth cruise ship on the way into our marina. I'm not much of a drinking man, but I was more than ready for a "sundowner" that evening. Janet's niece Kim joined us for a visit in Key West and we met up with an old friend who lives there. Quite a town—I don't believe there's another like it anywhere. We saw lots of interesting sights—but I'll save that for another story. After Kim left us, we moved on to more pedestrian Marathon and then on to Key Largo. Janet was thrilled to discover a family of manatees that lived under our pier in Key Largo. She wanted to get in the water with them until she saw the large crocodile that also lived nearby.

Time began to be a bit of an issue now. We had prearranged vacation visits from friends in Texas who wanted to sail with us, so we had to be in specific ports on specific days to meet them or drop them off. Also, hurricane season was in sight. I heard on the weather report that the first tropical depression had already begun to form in the Gulf. We moved more quickly up the east coast of Florida, but did stop long enough to enjoy Ft. Lauderdale, explore Coconut Grove, and visit the Space Center in Titusville. In a bit of lunacy, I got my ear pierced with a gold ring in Ft. Lauderdale on my 62nd birthday. I thought it made me look like a real sailor, and yes, I was sober at the time.

On June 2 we arrived in Brunswick, Georgia, where we had arranged to leave Sea Level for the rest of the summer. After four months, she had become a comfortable home to us and it was hard to leave her. Our plan was to return in the spring and begin what is called "The Great Loop," up the east coast of the United States, through part of Canada and the Great Lakes, and down the Mississippi River to the Gulf Coast. But, like all good plans, this one was destined to change.

Consequences of That Change

When we returned to Houston, we found that my mother had not fared well in our absence. She has never taken care of herself well, and this time was certainly no exception. She had become depressed while we were gone and had lost a great deal of weight, leaving her frailer than ever. Within days of our return, she overdosed on prescription painkillers and spent a night in the hospital. During that long night, I found myself experiencing a whole gamut of emotions — guilt, anger, sadness, even empathy. I understand her dislike of the change in status quo all too well. Her world is so limited because of her refusal to challenge her fears. We are her only support system, and she simply became overwhelmed when we were gone. Mom recovered rapidly after our return and things got back to normal for her.

Our greatest challenge was and still is balancing our responsibilities to my mother with our desire to live life to the fullest. I know that at times, I have used her as an excuse to delay things when in reality it was my own feelings of inadequacy that were to blame.

Janet and I are in agreement that we cannot, in good conscience, leave her alone again for an extended period. Our compromise is that we will continue our travels, but we will either take shorter trips or take her with us. She's quite an agreeable traveler, content to do almost anything within her physical capabilities or to occupy herself with television while she awaits our return. Because her physical limitations make it impossible to take her aboard a boat, we reluctantly made the decision to shelve our plans and put Sea Level on the market.

I wish I could report our four months of cruising were all bliss, but I am above all an honest man. We had some tense moments, some uncomfortable days and nights, some angry words and the worst fight we've ever had. We also had some glorious sailing, tranquil days, peaceful nights, and fabulous sex. We made new friends, visited new places, and saw old places in a new way. We solved problems as they arose, one at a time. We let time flow by at its own pace and rarely even looked at a watch. The journey left us closer than we've ever been and that alone was worth the trip.

Aboard Sea Level I did things I never would have attempted before and kept at them until I was successful — because I had to. There are few detours at sea and some scary passages are unavoidable. When things aboard the boat needed repair, I couldn't ignore them, put them off, or call someone else. My self-confidence grew with each success, and I found myself wondering why I'd been so afraid to try before. It's ironic that I was never afraid of failing athletically in front of a crowded stadium. In athletics, I always knew that I gave my best and — win or lose — that was good enough for me. I didn't give my best in other situations because I had no confidence. I've said that I didn't want to disappoint Janet; now I know that the one I didn't want to disappoint was me. There's no hiding from that.

My Current Status

Janet and I have always been friends, but the changes I've made have deepened our relationship and we enjoy being together more than ever before. Some people collect things and some collect experiences. We definitely fall into the latter category. A quote I keep handy is from Ernie J. Zelinski's great book *The Joy of Not Working*: "It's difficult to experience pleasure from reminiscing about things you haven't done." I know some people who get bored when their work life ends, but that has never been a problem for us. To get through the list of all the things we want to do would require several lifetimes.

I'm letting more in now and being more open with others. Several days a week, I do work I enjoy, teaching children with special needs. They get so much joy from simple things and are so connected to life even with the disabilities they have. I feel filled and refreshed after spending a day with them. I focus on staying in shape through regular exercise and enjoy playing golf. I've played for years, but now it's more about nurturing friendships rather than winning. I am genuinely pleased when a friend who is my opponent makes a good drive or a long putt. Where did the old guarded, competitive me go? I don't miss him. I am so grateful for this time in my life.

The best is now.

What Did I Learn?

I have learned so many things. To slow down, take time. To enjoy interesting conversation, good food, new friends, sunsets (and sunrises), good books. To relish small pleasures like clean sheets, a cool breeze, and the beauty of nature. To take a few risks. To trust myself. To rely on myself and not abdicate responsibility to others for fear of failure. Failure isn't the worst thing. Failure is still an experience. Not trying is the worst thing. It's amazing how creative you can be when you try. I've discovered how much enjoyment I can get out of just attempting something new. I've learned not to procrastinate as we never know how many tomorrows we may have. To live in the moment and not in the future. To pay attention and to be available to other people.

Anxiety and "what if" thinking keeps us stuck in the future, paralyzed and fearful. My decision to focus on the present has set me free. The only future thinking I do now is to anticipate our next adventure and know that whatever happens, happens. Now I say, bring it on. I'm ready.

Questions to Consider:

1. Are you living in the past, the present or the future?

2. If you knew you only had six months to live, what changes would you make in your life?

3. Recall an experience you remember vividly. What makes it so memorable?

4. Have you ever become so involved in an activity you lost track of time? What was that experience like for you?

5. Are you resistant to making changes or taking risks?

6. Is there something you would like to do but have not attempted because you think you might fail?

7. What does failure mean to you?

8. Who would be disappointed if you failed?

A Closing Thought From Ben and Ken

So many of us plan our lives around "one of these days." Instead of acting on our dreams we keep them just as dreams. As Henry David Thoreau put it, "Go confidently in the direction of your dreams. Live the life you have imagined." Mike's quote is equally relevant. "The best is now." He and Janet were willing to be risk takers in order to realize their dreams. Their bonus years are not just a future plan; they are making them happen now. Isn't that what dreams are for?

Chapter 4

BEYOND WORDS - READING BETWEEN THE LINES
Mary Arthur, Ed.D.

It was nine years after receiving my bachelor's degree and teaching certification that I decided to apply for my first teaching job. I had never intended to teach when I majored in home economics in college. Back then, careers for women seemed limited. Nursing and teaching were the favorite choices, and I really didn't want to do either. Home economics would give me the college degree I wanted, and would allow me to be a mom and homemaker while my husband supported our family.

Right out of college, I worked as a secretary while my husband Ken finished his master's degree. Three years later as he completed graduate school and began his first full-time job as a campus minister, I became pregnant with our first child. We made the decision together that I would be a stay-at-home mom. For our family, this was the right decision. Staying at home with my daughter and taking care of our home and family was a rewarding time in my life.

While pregnant with our second child, Ken made a career change and entered Air Force officer training, then pilot training. Our son was born the morning before my husband's pilot training class began. I was so grateful that this was my second child so I had a clue what to do! Fourteen- to 16-hour days of flying and studying consumed Ken's time, so I had the primary responsibility of caring for a new baby and a two-year-old. I absolutely enjoyed all of the time I had with my children.

Our first assignment after pilot training was to remain at the same base where Ken had earned his wings. He was selected to begin a three-year tour as an instructor pilot, and I was involved with the on-base life of an officer's wife. Even so, my children were the central core of my day-to-day living.

As we began the last year of this tour, I started thinking about the possibility of going back to work. Our son was old enough for preschool, and I had begun to consider the possibility that I might like to give teaching a try. There was an opening for a high school home economics teacher in the local school district, so I applied.

All my life I've had a philosophy that has proven to be true time after time. If I start feeling strongly about something, I act on it. Central to this belief is a conviction that God leads us and opens opportunities for us. The other half of this belief is that it is our job to keep our eyes open, to be alert to the opportunities that are there, and to respond to those opportunities. Obviously, if I didn't apply for the job, there was no possibility for me to get it. With more than a little trepidation, I filled out the application at the school district office.

To be honest, I definitely had doubts I could even perform the duties of a teacher. It had been nine years since I had received my teaching certification, and I was sure much had changed in education. Could I remember how to do lesson plans? Did I still have the content knowledge I needed?

I was offered the job and made the decision to take it. I told the personnel director up front that I would only be there for one year because I knew that our family would be moved by the Air Force the following summer.

That first year of teaching was remarkable. I was in a great school with five other home economics teachers. One other teacher was also in her first year, so we spent time planning our lessons together. I learned so much from those teachers, and was grateful for the opportunity to gain some experience. Looking back, that experience gave me a solid foundation for the teaching positions I would have later.

It is so great to look back on the experiences that you were not sure about at the time and be able to see how they fit into the big scheme of your life! Every experience we have adds something to who we are. I often wonder about how my current experiences are preparing me for something that I will need in my future. Inevitably I will be able to look back and see it!

Our next Air Force assignment took us overseas to England. I applied to teach at the Department of Defense schools and got a job as a middle school English teacher. The DOD school system required only that you have a teaching certificate in any subject and at least 18 hours in the subject you taught. I loved English in college, so I took a couple of electives in addition to the required hours. I guess I was being prepared at that time to be able to get the teaching job in England. There were no home economics courses in the DOD schools, so English was the only subject I could teach there.

That second year of teaching wasn't as remarkable as the first. I had the content knowledge, but no pedagogical knowledge for teaching English, especially at middle school. The position started six weeks into the school year when the current teacher had decided to retire. Starting with an established class is very difficult for an inexperienced teacher. Discipline was not established and it took me most of the year to have any meaningful classroom management. I kept thinking, "Why am I doing this? This is too hard and I don't like middle school students!" I felt that they didn't appreciate all of the planning and effort I was making to help them learn the wonderful world of literature, grammar and spelling!

At the end of that year, I decided not to return as a full-time teacher and instead to work in the fall as a substitute at the DOD high school. This was not a difficult decision, because it allowed me a great deal of flexible time to travel with the Officers' Wives' Club on some great short European trips. I thoroughly enjoyed substituting for high school English classes. It renewed my confidence as a teacher and my ability to manage a classroom. Following the lesson plans of experienced teachers taught me some methods of teaching the content that were engaging and effective for students.

At the end of three and a half years in England, my husband and I once again made the challenging decision to change careers. The airlines were hiring and the time was right for Ken to end his Air Force career. After a long and arduous process, he was hired by a major airline before we even left England, so it was only a couple of weeks between jobs.

I have always supported my husband in his decisions to change careers. It seems a little scary to make a change from a known, secure job with a regular paycheck, but my "follow your heart" philosophy seems to always pay off for us. Each career move has opened new doors and provided great life experiences for our family. I think it is wrong to discourage those you love from trying a new direction for their life even if there are uncertainties about the future. I do know in my heart that we have always been able to look back and discover why we were led in a certain direction.

These career changes were always good times for our marriage. My support for my husband's choices was a way I could show my love for him and my confidence in him. It actually came easily for me since I always viewed change as an exciting new adventure that I would understand in retrospect. Every time that happened, it made it easier to step out on faith the next time!

We knew while still in England that we would be living in the Dallas, Texas, area so I sent applications to several suburban school districts that I had heard were good districts. As soon as we arrived back in the States, I started calling to see if there were openings for home economics teachers. It was July, so I found that most of the districts had no more openings for any teaching positions.

One phone call led me to a middle school where there was an opening for an English teacher. My stomach went into a knot. "Lord, are you really going to make me teach middle school students again?" The school secretary I was talking with said the principal was at the administration building at that very moment looking through applications and that I should call her there. I did, and she told me that she had just set my application aside because I didn't have a certification in English. I assured her that I had taught English at the DOD schools, and was willing to do whatever I needed to become certified. Though I didn't have a Texas certification for teaching English, because I had taught it for that year in the Department of Defense schools, I was considered for the position. I interviewed with the principal and felt strongly that this would be a good choice. It was an opportunity that came my way and I knew I could not ignore it. Even though I was afraid that I wouldn't be able to teach middle school, I stepped out on faith and accepted the job when it was offered.

I taught English for the next five years at that school, and even got to instruct a couple of sections of the home economics courses! Because of that one year of educating in England, I had the opportunity to teach at a wonderful school where I learned to love middle school students! They were fun, full of curiosity, and very interested in learning when lessons were well planned and engaging. I learned so much during those years and taught with some incredible teachers who were willing to share ideas and collaborate. During these years, I encountered a number of students who had trouble reading even after a great deal of instruction. I was concerned about them but really didn't know what to do to help them learn to read more effectively. My principal encouraged me to take some master's classes in reading. This encouragement let me to complete a master's degree with a reading specialist certification.

The last year of graduate school, I resigned my teaching position so that I could pursue the master's full-time. I worked part-time in the district as an induction year liaison, and enjoyed the responsibility of mentoring first year teachers as they refined their teaching skills. It was very fulfilling work, and I realized how much I would enjoy a career of educating and supporting other teachers.

I was fortunate my husband's airline career was "taking off" and he was receiving increases in salary as his experience level and years of service grew. This gave me the opportunity to decrease my salary temporarily while I completed my master's degree. During my last semester, one of my professors encouraged me to apply for a doctoral fellowship with the university.

I had just begun learning all of the theories of reading instruction and it was helping me understand how ineffective I had been in helping adolescents who were struggling readers. I wanted to learn more! Beginning a doctoral program was a daunting task, however. It would be a very hard, long, and expensive process. I wasn't sure it would be fair to my family for me to spend money on my further education. By now, both of my children were in high school. We had been saving to send them to college since they were babies, but I wasn't sure we could also afford for me to be in graduate school at the same time.

My husband encouraged me to apply for the doctoral fellowship. In keeping with my lifelong philosophy, I reasoned to myself that if I didn't get the fellowship, it would be an indication I wasn't meant to keep going to school, and if I did, I was to continue on.

This isn't a laissez-faire attitude where I think, "What happens just happens." Instead, it means to do everything that you have control over to open the opportunities, then trust that the things out of your control will happen as they are meant to. I had control over putting in my application for the doctoral fellowship on time, interviewing with the committee, and praying for guidance. The committee's decision was out of my control, so I couldn't worry about that part.

I was awarded the doctoral fellowship for three years, so I thought, "Oh, great! Now I have to do a doctorate, write a dissertation, and take statistics." What was I thinking? Here I was in my mid forties and about to start the most challenging academic program. But knowing that God had provided this opportunity for me gave me the confidence that he would be with me all the way. The fellowship provided an income for three years so I could take the doctoral courses full time. I loved taking the advanced classes. They were challenging, stimulating, and taught me more than I ever imagined about the complex process of how children learn to read.

My final year of the program was the dissertation process. I wanted to work once again in a school district so that I would be able to teach adolescents and complete my dissertation study. Once again, I saw how prior experiences prepared me for a new situation. The director of the Induction Year Liaison program that I worked with in my previous school district was now an assistant superintendent in another district close by our new home. By looking on their website for job openings, I discovered they had posted available positions for reading specialists. At the end of my master's degree, I had received an all level reading specialist certification, so this was a wonderful opportunity. I applied, was interviewed, hired, and placed at a middle school once again. This time I was a reading specialist with the charge of helping struggling readers and working with their teachers to promote good reading instruction.

I completed my dissertation study of effective one-on-one reading instruction for adolescents. I did my study with two struggling readers who were in eighth grade. They had never passed the state reading test and had a great deal of trouble in all of their classes because of their poor reading ability. After working with them for a semester using all of the strategies I had learned in my master's and doctoral courses, they both showed significant growth in their reading levels and both passed the eighth grade state reading test. To me, this was one of the most fulfilling experiences I have ever had as a teacher.

My doctorate was completed at the end of the third year of my fellowship. After three more years of working as a reading specialist, I was offered the position of coordinator of language arts and reading for the entire school district. All of my experiences teaching and learning in the past 19 years had prepared me for this new job.

I can look back now after five years in this position and see clearly specific things that happened to me, specific training I attended, books I read, and people who mentored me, and know that they all contributed to the knowledge and skills I have to make this career meaningful for me. I am able to work with teachers to improve literacy instruction in all grade levels. I work with a wonderful group of directors, coordinators, and principals in a collaborative environment. I am continuously growing.

I don't know what future changes I will have in my life, but I expect that there will be many. My two children are grown and involved with their careers. They both completed college degrees and are finding their own pathways in life.

I still give them advice to follow their hearts and to not be afraid of making changes. My husband recently started a new career once again. He took early retirement from the airline and began the first eight-to-five job he has ever had in his life. It's an exciting time for our entire family.

There are two verses from the Bible that have guided my choices in life. In Matthew 7:7, Jesus said, "Ask, and it will be given to you; seek and you will find; knock, and the door will be opened to you." David said in Psalm 56:3-4, "When I am afraid, I will trust in you. In God, whose word I praise, in God I trust; I will not be afraid. What can mortal man do to me?" I know that if I trust in God and seek out opportunities in life, I won't be disappointed. I can't be afraid of what might happen but trust that God will be with me in the decisions he leads me to make. God wants us to live joyous, abundant lives. That doesn't mean that everything will always be perfect. I have had difficult and sad times in my life. Those experiences have also contributed to who I am and the strength that I have.

My eyes are always open to new opportunities, and I look forward to looking back some day to see how the experiences I am having right now have prepared me for a future I have not even imagined.

A Closing Thought From Ben and Ken

Mary's way of looking at life brings her tremendous peace. She's willing to consider any changes that come her way because of her faith in God's leadership and her willingness to take risks. Some people just wait for opportunities to present themselves. They live in a state of passivity and rarely reach their full potential. Mary, instead, set high expectations for herself and then worked to open doors of opportunities. Some people see themselves as "too old" for formal education. She saw her bonus years as an opportunity to reach her full academic potential. Age was not a barrier—it was a plus. She had experience and maturity in her academic pursuit that made the experience better. Mary lives her bonus years as a great adventure that she's still discovering. What an exciting way to view life!

For you, education might not be in a university setting. It might be learning a skill you've always desired ... getting a pilot's license, taking a dog training course, earning a scuba certification, enrolling in a real estate license seminar, learning to play golf or tennis or a musical instrument.

Whatever you've always wanted to do but felt you were too old to accomplish, recognize what Mary did: it's not too late. These are the bonus years! Open the doors of opportunity and reach for your dreams.

NON TRADITIONAL – WHO SAYS?
Don Andrews

I have spent most of my life in or around sports at various stages, starting with Little League and Pop Warner to the elite levels of hockey, rodeo, ski racing and motor sports. It has been enjoyable, for the most part, and a respectable way to earn a living. However, I have always been perplexed by the term people use to describe the sports I love: "non-traditional." What is non-traditional to one person may well be traditional and customary to another. If you reside in the United States of America, football is traditional and soccer may be considered somewhat non-traditional. If you live in the rest of the world, "futbol" is traditional and American football is quite unique.

I have not really experienced the traditional life in sports or my business career. When I was twelve years old I started playing ice hockey. It was the first year of youth hockey in a hot-bed of hockey, Nashville, Tennessee — yea, right! A minor league professional team had come to town a few years earlier and I thought it was a very cool game — no pun intended. It was a lot of fun and I was the only kid at my school playing the game. But, it was considered a non-traditional sport at that time, especially in the South.

When I was fourteen I started SCUBA diving with the "gang" I ran with at school; we grew up together and were all in the high school band so it was not a drive-by shooting type gang. When I was 16, I started racing a quarter midget (small open-wheel race car) that belonged to the father of a girl I was dating. That was really fun until I broke up with her and my racing career took a major setback. When I was 18, I started sky diving, which is a real rush, literally. This is a true adrenaline sport but balanced on the "blind scale" by the possibility, however remote, of mortal accidents. This was my first personal introduction to the psychological personality trait of "sensation seekers," which would play an important role in my professional life. When I was 21, I started flying airplanes. I figured if I was going to jump out of a perfectly good airplane I might as well learn how to fly them also.

I liked golf, tennis, water skiing and playing stick-and-ball "traditional" sports when I was growing up, but everybody did that. For some reason I enjoyed doing things that most people didn't do and/or didn't want to do. It was no different in my professional life. I went to the University of Tennessee to become a physical therapist but got into professional hockey as a back-up goaltender and athletic trainer and did not go to graduate school to complete the physical therapy degree. This decision would have a much greater impact on my business career than I could imagine at the time.

Life is full of choices; it also provides us with detours and roadblocks over which we have absolutely no control. With experience (and age) one begins to realize some things are just meant to be and others are not. From a religious perspective, God has a plan for all of us but most of the time he keeps it a secret. God must have a real sense of humor, watching us fumble around down here trying to figure it all out, especially when he knows we rarely will.

I fell in love with the game of hockey as a kid and made a living in the sport for many years after college. While working for the New York Islanders Hockey Club of the National Hockey League (NHL), I went to Fort Worth, Texas, as the head athletic trainer with their development team in the Central Hockey League. As I was responsible for the physical well-being of the players the Islanders sent to Fort Worth, I needed a good orthopedic surgeon/team physician to evaluate and diagnose our players' injuries. Through a friend who was one of the athletic trainers with the Dallas Cowboys football team, I met J. Pat Evans, M.D., who was their team physician. I asked Dr. Evans if he would see our hockey players and he agreed to do so. A couple of years later he asked me if I would assist him covering an elite invitational professional rodeo being held in our arena in Fort Worth. I did, and thus began a new and challenging chapter in my life.

Hockey players are tough individuals, but I had never worked with athletes as resistant to pain and adverse conditions as rodeo cowboys. After the event was over I asked Dr. Evans what kind of event medical coverage this group of athletes had during the regular season, and he said none or very little. The wheels started turning … "Tough athletes, sensation seekers, great group of highly motivated patients with little or no continuity of medical care common to the more traditional team sports" … a unique opportunity was at hand. But why take the risk? I already had a career in professional sports with security, retirement and all the trappings that come with being involved with professional athletes.

Was there an existing diagram or business plan to follow to establish medical coverage for professional rodeo athletes? Absolutely not! I would have to start from scratch. But there was certainly a unique opportunity at hand. We had "demand;" now we just needed to formulate the "supply."

Over the next few months Dr. Evans and I wrote and rewrote the concept of mobile sports medicine for organizations governing individual athletes. With the support of the director of the "Rodeo Super Stars" event we had just covered, Walt Garrison (both a Dallas Cowboy and rodeo cowboy), and Donnie Gay (eight time world bull riding champion), we took the concept to the Professional Rodeo Cowboys Association in Colorado Springs for a test drive. The administration of the PRCA, the pro rodeo sanctioning body, liked the idea and said, "Let's try this out at the National Finals Rodeo in December," which happens to be the "Super Bowl" of the sport of rodeo.

A couple of months later we contacted the Justin Boot Company who came on board as the title sponsor to completely fund the first mobile sports medicine program in North America. This was crucial as the service would be gratis to every contestant, thus the Justin Sportsmedicine Team was born. We covered 11 events that first year and now we cover well over 150 rodeo events annually.

About ten years later a number of the bull riders in pro rodeo started a new segment of the industry and asked us to provide medical coverage; this was the beginning of the Professional Bull Riders (PBR) Series. Bull riders certainly needed the service as they have the highest injury rate in rodeo (almost 50 percent of treated injuries) and probably the highest major injury rate of any professional athlete worldwide.

The professional rodeo program was an instant success because of the demand for comprehensive sports medicine care and the fact that we were able to supply a program that met their specific need. I thought to myself, if this concept could be successful in one "non-traditional" sport, why not others.

As a kid I had loved motor racing from the first time I listened to the Indianapolis 500 and Darlington, South Carolina Southern 500 on radio. As I mentioned, I did a little racing until I lost my ride—broke up with the car owner's daughter—and knew it was a rugged and dangerous sport at the professional level. If the rodeo program could be successful, why couldn't a similar program work in elite motor sports?

We followed the same business model, went to two experts in the field and presented a "plan" to the sanctioning body of Indy Car Racing. Johnny Rutherford, three time Indy 500 champion, and Wally Dallenbach, retired Indy car driver and chief steward of the sanctioning organization, supported our concept, and four years after the rodeo program began we brought mobile sports medicine to the world of auto racing. Our first official event was the United States Grand Prix, one of 16 races that make up the FIA Formula One World Championship. One of our first patients was a rookie driver from Brazil by the name of Ayrton Senna who went on to be, arguably, the best driver to ever sit in a race car in any series around the world. He was a tremendous athlete and became an advocate of our program up until his untimely death at the San Marino Grand Prix in Imola, Italy.

As in rodeo, the motor sports program was an immediate success as we had supplied a much needed service to a physical and demanding sport. In the early '90s we introduced the mobile sports medicine concept at the NASCAR (National Association of Stock Car Auto Racing) level with the help of a good friend, Jeff Hammond, a racer and a rodeo cowboy who had won three Winston Cup Championships as a crew chief, and Davey Allison, a second generation driving champion and vocal supporter of safety and medical care in stock car racing. With the new millennium we introduced the program to the elite level of world sports car racing when we provided the service to the American Le Mans Series. These are the same cars and drivers that compete at the prestigious 24 Hours of Le Mans in France each June.

Now for those of you who may not consider driving a race car an athletic endeavor, let me assure you driving an 800 horsepower race car without adequate fluid breaks, in a fire protection suit that does not vent heat, in a cockpit where temperatures reach 140 degrees for hours on end, with no regular time-outs and with heart rates approaching 180 beats a minute—these are athletes. They have the same needs as all the "traditional" athletes. A major difference in motor sports and in rodeo is that a mistake made in these sports can be catastrophic.

If you make an error in stick and ball sports like dropping a ball in the outfield or in the end zone, you may get booed by the fans or chastised by the coaches, but in rodeo and motor sports you will pay a much higher price for your mistakes. In numerous years of hockey coverage I had one scary incident when a player slid head first into the end boards behind the goaltenders net. Luckily he was fine and played the next day. During my tenure in rodeo and motor sports, 21 athletes I have worked with have lost their lives competing in the sport they love so much.

Why do they do it? In a word: passion! They love what they do. It is not for the money. All will tell you, whether man or woman, that it is not about the money. They do it for the love of the game, the rush of being on the ragged edge of the envelope. When they have been there once they want to go there again and again and again. It is a "sensation" most of us will never experience, but once we do (so they say), we will seek to go there again and again. They have a complete blast racing side-by-side at 200 miles per hour or riding a bull or a bucking horse that has never been ridden before. The passion for their game is so intense that even when they are in a wreck they want to do it again. I have had many drivers tell me while flipping end over end or sliding upside down on their head, they are thinking, "When this piece of junk stops, I will make this and that adjustment to the back-up car as soon as we can get it out of the trailer and get back out on the track." Rodeo cowboys who have just been kicked, stepped on, hooked by a horn or mashed to a pulp in the bucking chutes want to know when they can get back on to ride again. We haven't even completed our initial patient evaluation—much less diagnosis, prognosis, treatment plan or paperwork—and they want to know if they can take their reride or get on a "real good one" tomorrow night!

These athletes have a passion for what they do in life. If you are willing to "pay the price," then you too can seek this sensation from your chosen endeavor. But without passion and commitment you will just be in another job. I have heard on many occasions the expression, "Happy people are not afraid of dying; they are afraid of not living." John Eldredge pointed out in his book *Wild at Heart*, "Don't ask yourself what the world needs. Ask what makes you come alive, and go do that, because what the world needs is people who have come alive."

I targeted sports and groups of athletes that were considered non-traditional in the eyes of most people because I knew these people were full of life and would be very interesting to work with. I have not been disappointed after many years of working with and learning from these exceptional athletes and patients. I could have played it safe and stayed in the traditional stick and ball sports or the clinical setting working with typical medical patients. I chose to venture into an unknown realm of medicine with the thought that "this could really be interesting" and there certainly is a need for traditional sports medicine services in these so-called "non-traditional" sports. You can do this as well; you just need to take the first step.

One of the first commandments of business is that "seldom does anything happen on your schedule." You want to complete a contract or close a negotiation within a specific timeline and it just doesn't work out that way. With experience you learn to accept this fact, and the sooner the better. This particular mandate, however, does not diminish the other "laws" or the "steps" to business success, of which we shall discuss in just a minute.

I declared a double degree path in college—science (pre-physical therapy curriculum) and business. I took the traditional business courses but very few professors or instructors emphasized the number one priorities of business success: dedication, persistence and hard work. Very hard work.

One of the best resources for the emerging entrepreneur is "the classics" of the business book world. I will date myself with these selections but I believe in the KISS Principle and would highly recommend some books that have been around for a while. Robert Townsend's *Up the Organization* (and sequel, *Further Up the Organization*), Mark McCormick's *What They Don't Teach You at Harvard Business School* and the "primer" for anyone in any business, Harry Lorayne and Jerry Lucas' *The Memory Book*. The Lorayne/Lucas method of memorization is without a doubt the best way to remember individuals' names if you are willing to apply the principles of the authors.

If you want a more current text and a very good read on making great business deals (or even little ones), you might pick up a copy of *The Biggest Game of All* by Leo Hindery, Jr. The author is probably not a household name to most, but Leo is one of the most interesting people I have ever met. Leo has lunch and plays golf with Ted Turner, Tiger Woods, Rupert Murdock, Bill Gates and a long list of others in the business and entertainment world. That being said, Leo is one of the most down-to-earth guys you will ever meet. He was a patient of mine in sports car racing and actually has a podium finish (top three teams) at the 24 Hours of Le Mans in France. You will enjoy his unique path to business success as Leo is anything but traditional.

Personally, I get a kick out of the countless business books that lament the "number of steps" to success. Some that come to mind are: *The 21 Irrefutable Laws...*, *The 16 Timeless Principles ...*, *The Dozen Principles ...*, *The 10 Simple Secrets ...*, *The 7 Habits...*, and a myriad of other literary titles you would also recognize. These are interesting and the authors have all achieved a certain level of success or report on individuals or companies who have enjoyed business success. These related works represent good reading but could be reduced to a much smaller and more manageable number of steps.

There are three steps to being successful in business, and these steps are absolute. Incidentally the first two steps are the basic laws of entry level economics—the simple laws of supply and demand. Number one, research the marketplace. Is there a need (demand)? Number two, establish a business plan; fill the need (supply). And number three, work your butt off. The first two are really not that difficult to construct but the third is what separates the men from the boys, the women from the girls, the wheat from the chaff, the ...well, you get the point. This is the greatest barrier to entry for most businesses and for most people who wish to start a business, be it traditional or not.

So, are you willing to give what it takes? Are you willing to make the sacrifices necessary to achieve the desired results? Most people aren't and here lies the greatest "niche" for success. Research indicates it takes approximately five years to break even or show a profit in a new business. Can you afford the economic plight and the time commitment to follow a five year plan? If you can't, it might be best to stay right where you are. We are talking about 50-, 60- and even 70-hour work weeks for up to five years and maybe more. Hard work is what will separate you from the pack and it doesn't require a bachelor's, master's or doctorate degree. What it does require is something you better already have—a very strong work ethic.

If you follow the first two steps and are willing to work extremely hard, you can achieve anything. And yes, I mean anything and at any age. Why get stuck in a traditional job when the world is full of undiscovered opportunities? Step number one is a vast land of unexplored options, and as our population grows and ages there will be a plethora of consumer and/or industry "demands." It will be up to the entrepreneur to initiate the "supply" mechanism in a timely and productive manner. Small business will thrive in the future as the world virtually shrinks due to multiple technologies, especially forms of mass communication. In business as well as in personal relationships, communication is the basis for long term success. If you can get your clear and precise message to the consumer in a quick and reliable manner, you will reap the reward. This is the advantage of being small and nimble in the business equation versus being large and encumbered. This David versus Goliath scenario in business quite often has the same results as reported in the book of 1 Samuel in the Old Testament. But it will require a tremendous amount of determination because you are small and "they" are the behemoth.

Many people refer to "big" as traditional and this is good for us as it opens the door for what is referred to as the non-traditional (in their minds) business venture. Find the niche (demand), create a plan (supply) and then beat the rest to the desired results. Do this because you can ... and you want to ... and you are willing to work harder than the others.

Another component of success that is critically important is persistence. Without it, when the going gets tough—and trust me it will—you might just throw in the towel and say you gave it the old college try. When you run into the inevitable road block, you make a minor correction and keep heading toward your stated objective. Calvin Coolidge said it best: "Nothing in the world can take the place of persistence. Talent will not; nothing is more common than unsuccessful men with talent. Genius will not; unrewarded genius is almost a proverb. Education will not; the world is full of educated derelicts. Persistence and determination alone are omnipotent. The slogan 'Press on' has solved and always will solve the problems of the human race."

Again we need to emphasize passion as a key element not to be overlooked. This is essential and is a critical element of step number three. For an example, it would be foolhardy to embark on this journey if money is the only incentive. You had better love what you are doing or you will not be able to endure the 50 to 70 hours a week that are required for success.

You may already have that passion for something but may not have contemplated how to turn a specific aspect of your passion into a viable business entity. Feel your passion, follow your heart and you can quite possibly create and succeed in a non-traditional business. I did, so why not you? I am neither super intelligent, highly educated, a business whiz kid, a recipient of a trust fund, multi-talented or any other quality that predisposes me to business success. I had a passion and turned it into a successful business venture. You will have to decide if it was traditional or non-traditional because I already know.

Why me? Why not someone before me? As I stated earlier, I am not exceptional in any regard except that I was willing to take a chance and follow a passion. Did I really take that big of a chance? I don't think so because I followed the simple principles of supply and demand. No, it had never been done before, but should you "follow where the path may lead or go instead where there is no path and leave a trail?" Another popular expression states, "You cannot discover new oceans unless you have the courage to lose sight of the shore."

As we age we have a tendency to "reside" in our comfort zone or stay with the things that are familiar and relatively safe. Is this truly living? Now is a great time to branch out and try something new. Is it risky? It all depends on what you try to accomplish! There is very little reward without some risk, although we all want to manage risk, whether it is in the stock market, our daily lives or a new business adventure. Just remember—nothing ventured, nothing gained!

Starting a new business does not have to be a roulette wheel gamble where you put your wager on the table and hope the little ball stops in the slot you selected. If you carefully follow the basic business plan of niche marketing (target market supply and demand) in an area of personal passion with total commitment, persistence and hard work, I will virtually guarantee that you will succeed. The most important part—you will never know if you don't try. What is life without adventure? Again, John Eldredge says in *Wild At Heart*, "Life is not a problem to be solved; it is an adventure to be lived." You will never regret it, but you may be disappointed if you never tried.

There is no time limit on taking a leap of faith, regardless of your age. Build your confidence with preparation and then "Just Do It." Phil Knight of Nike fame made a fortune by taking a "non-traditional" approach to the shoe industry. Was it a big gamble? If you ask Phil I bet he would tell you he was following his passion with a sound business plan. We may not all start a company that reaches the world renown level of a Nike, but we can achieve the personal satisfaction of blazing a unique trail. That is, if we are willing to follow the basics and commit the time, energy and persistence required. Look in the mirror and ask yourself, "Am I willing to make the sacrifices necessary now that I know what I want to do?" Only you can answer that question!

My favorite business quotation comes from one of the brightest men in management who just so happens to be a great football coach, Vince Lombardi. "The quality of a person's life is in direct proportion to their commitment to excellence, regardless of their chosen field of endeavor." Another Coach Lombardi quote I feel is most significant to our discussion is, "If you believe in yourself and have the courage, the determination, the dedication, the competitive drive and if you are willing to sacrifice the little things in life and pay the price for the things that are worthwhile, it can be done." As I mentioned earlier, I did not finish my physical therapy degree, which presented some barriers in the traditional medical career path. However, that made me even more determined to succeed because of my passion for the endeavor. I was determined to win regardless of the roadblocks.

I have always been intrigued that the quote most often attributed to Coach Lombardi is, quite frankly, almost always misquoted. He never said, "Winning is not everything, *it is the only thing*." What he actually said, which is much more profound, was, "Winning is not everything, but making the effort to win is."

If you have spent most of your life in sports, business or any endeavor, it is never too late to make a navigational correction. You just have to muster the courage to "make the leap" and then never look back. Follow the simple but critical steps and be willing to sacrifice the things necessary for step number three. If you make the effort and commit to these philosophies, you cannot lose, regardless of your chosen field of endeavor!

A Closing Thought From Ben and Ken

Don had a passion for sports that could easily have taken him down many different paths. Instead, he lived the truth of Robert Frost's "The Road Less Traveled" and Emerson's ideas of individualism. Don developed his zest for sports into a business that has helped athletes in different sports around the world. He forged a path into an area where no one had ventured. His bonus years are being spent in a field he loves, with people who are exciting, and performing a service that is totally unique. In selecting "non-traditional" sports, he found the perfect niche for his talents.

In considering your bonus years, don't overlook the roads less traveled. Consider the opportunities that may seem offbeat or distinctive. You may find that you have a gift, talent, or creativity that has been ignored and is perfect for some opportunity in your path.

STEPPING OUT IN THE MIDST OF CHANGE
Stacey Condit Campbell

Change is the law of life.
And those who look only to the past or present
are certain to miss the future.
—John F. Kennedy

Introduction

At a church retreat, a 40-something girlfriend was describing what she did for a living and ended with, "…but I am trying to figure out what I want to be now that I am all grown up." She described a new magazine she gives as a gift to other women who are turning 40. The magazine highlights life after 40 and the changes people make late in their lives. It seems many of us are looking for that something more out of life as we enter our "mature years." Stay-at-home mothers like me, I think, especially find a need to reinvent themselves as their children enter school full time or graduate and move on to college. It is a defining moment for a mother who has devoted her life to raising kids. There is a moment when you realize this part of your life is over and that "What next?" question begins to creep into the foreground much more than it did when you were busy as a soccer mom, PTA mom, church leader or in some other role that revolved around your children.

When I was asked to contribute to this book, I grappled with what to say—how have I dealt with the change in my life, especially at mid-life? As a woman, it seems that change is inherently natural and an incredible part of being female. Change for a woman is also socially defined in so many anecdotal ways: reaching adolescence and "becoming a woman;" graduating high school and choosing a career that can or should be set aside for a family some day; finding a mate at the right age (not too young, which is foolish, and not too old, which makes us spinsters); settling down into a marriage where the role of a woman has been passed down through the ages; having children (not before marriage preferably); becoming a mother. That seems to complete our life cycle then. Life seems to somewhat end there—at becoming a mother. Then our role is to be a good wife, mother, citizen, which all somehow intertwine to form the web of our lives for a good while or until a portion of that webbing is broken—the children are grown, our spouse takes ill or passes. Then suddenly we are not so certain anymore about who we are or what our purpose is. We feel a bit lost as our definitions are removed and we are left standing alone. Sociologists often refer to this as a "roleless role."

My mother is in that predicament. A devoted wife, mother of three, and citizen of the year, who now—after all the children are grown, moved away and with families of their own, and the sudden death of my father at age 59—is left undefined. She has not taken well to trying to reinvent herself at this late stage in life. She never took care of herself with all the mothering and caring she did for others and now doesn't know who she is. It has been over 10 years since my father's passing and still she seems stuck in this place. She makes the excuse that her health is not good. Even though she has been diagnosed with emphysema, she continues to smoke. She tells us, her children, that she would be happier if we visited more or lived closer—still caught in the mothering, parenting mode. She will probably never reach her full potential past being a wife and mother. As a daughter, that is very hard to watch. I try to motivate her to change, to get out and make new friends, to see all that she has left to give and do with her life, but to no avail.

My History

My brothers and I were born and raised in rural northern New

Jersey. I am the middle child and only girl in the family. My mother was a stay-at-home mom who never graduated high school but was very active in the community. My father, a high school graduate, began work at age 18 at Bristol Myers Company, eventually working his way up the corporate ladder to a supervisor's position. Our lives were rich in that we had devoted, loving parents who taught us to be good stewards of the earth and good citizens, caring of our neighbors.

We had a beautiful home in the woods and many friends. My father loved to garden and be in the woods, and my mother kept up our home while helping and supporting us to become poised, well-mannered, faithful children. However, being the only daughter in my family, I found that there were different rules of the house that applied to me "for my protection and well-being" as my parents would often explain. As a Jersey girl growing up in the '70s and '80s, I did not appreciate being predefined and so I worked at not completely conforming to old-fashioned notions of what a good girl's role in a family or community was.

My mother assigned me typical "girl" jobs of cleaning up dishes, dusting and vacuuming, when I really wanted to be outside helping my dad plant the vegetable garden or change the oil in the car. I do not think I was a "rebel" as I loved and respected my parents, teachers and others who were there to guide me along the way. I knew the rebellious teen was not the road I wanted to take. I just wanted to find myself, who I was, who I wanted to be, and work toward that goal.

Church helped me as a teen to realize some of who I did and did not want to be. My parents were not churchgoers as my father was raised Catholic and my mother Presbyterian, yet neither was enamored by organized religions. However, my brothers and I were still raised to be faithful. Prayer was part of our daily lives. So, when I got my driver's license, I decided to go to church on my own. I explored many religions during my teen and early college years by visiting various churches with friends. Truly, I feel the church helped keep me from going "wild" as a young adult finding that first taste of freedom from parental supervision. At least I knew what I did not want to be.

When my father lost his job at age 50, everything changed for us as a family. We had to sell our home, our boat, our RV, all of which held so many family memories. We had to move and leave all the friends we had grown to love and depend on and redefine our lives. I begged to be left behind to complete my last year of high school with my class. Reluctantly, my mother and father agreed and I lived with my boyfriend's parents for a few months.

I was on my own now as they both worked; my family was in Florida, and my boyfriend was off at college all week. It was a huge time of personal growth for me to take control of these new circumstances, decide what I wanted to study in college and determine how I was going to pay for it with my family's financial situation in a shambles. My parents had chosen to live out their "dream life" in Naples, Florida. They always cherished our vacations to Florida and thought this was the best place to move.

Soon, they invested my father's retirement funds into some rental property and the remainder in a retail store. This is when the retail market went dry, and my parents lost most of their life savings. I just finished college at Florida International University and landed my first good job, my oldest brother was a lawyer and married with his first child, and my youngest brother was entering college when my father died of a massive heart attack. Again, suddenly, our lives were being redefined. This time my mother did not have the strength to redefine herself without her husband by her side.

My father's death was painful for me as I was very close to him. He seemed the only one who really understood me. I was angry with him for dying and at God for taking him. In the midst of my own anguish, I was also trying to be supportive of my mother in her heartbreak and make sense of all these new definitions thrust upon us. As I was busily trying to figure out all this newness, I watched my mother flounder as a single woman in her 50s. I was also grappling with the loss of what I held dear and the emotional upheaval left behind. My life had changed in a way that I was not expecting. And, once again, I found myself reevaluating life's purpose and what my role was in it. It was then that I told myself I will not let that happen to me — I will not be so lost in all the definitions that I can no longer find myself.

When I got back to work, I saw an article about an organization that helped busy working people get involved in their communities. Miami in the '90s was a place that was filled with killings, child abductions, Hurricane Andrew stories, and other horrors that I was amazed I had escaped during my 10 years there. If any place needed its citizens to be more involved, it was there, so I inquired. As it happened, someone else thought the same and was trying to pull together a board of directors to get this volunteer organization started in Miami. It was then that I became the founding vice president for Hands On Miami, an organization dedicated to building a better community through volunteerism. Finally, I had found my purpose. Sure, I had a wonderful job at the John S. and James L. Knight Foundation, but I also now was able to help those in need, help people redefine themselves to get to a better place, and educate those with the resources to realize their ability to help make Miami a better place to live. It was idyllic and I loved it. I spent most of my free time working with a dynamic group of young adults to grow this exciting new organization.

Then, my husband Doug entered the picture. He was a sweet, caring yet rugged Ph.D. chemist who was working for the University of Miami's oceanographic department.

This was another defining point in my life. I was now a wife and soon, a mother. As I adjusted to these new roles, I tried to keep in mind the early life lessons gifted to me from my parents.

I attempted to continue working even after my first child was born but realized my work was to be a mother at this time, so I left my job. It seemed my life was being redefined on almost a weekly basis once I graduated college, got my first job, lost a parent, became a wife and now had become a mother to a beautiful baby girl. My life, I realized, was no longer my own. Should I be afraid of this? How should I deal with this? How can I be sure not to lose my sense of self in all this change?

My husband got a job offer in the Seattle area. The roots I grew in Miami were being transplanted once again. It was tough as a new mother, learning how to cope with this new and very important job without friends or family nearby for many hours, even by plane. I had to do this on my own and because I had no other involvements or commitments in this new city, I was able to concentrate my efforts on being a wife and mother.

I looked for other mothers and joined a school for toddlers and parents that offered parenting classes and a chance to interact with other moms who seemed to be trying to figure out their new jobs as well. Some were working moms, some sent their nannies to fill in as a parent, and still others were in my position—a full-time mom. Again, I keenly observed what I was sure I did not want to be. As a child, my mother was always there for me when I needed her, and I planned to be there for my daughter too. This was my definition for now and I was okay with that.

My second beautiful daughter was born. We took every opportunity as a family to enjoy the majestic beauty Washington State had to offer by going on hikes, having picnics, riding the ferry, enjoying the fresh air and scrumptious seafood, getting glimpses of whales, sipping on Starbucks or Seattle's Best coffees. My girls learned about Indian culture, banana slugs and spawning salmon. We connected to a church home there as well. It was wonderful. But, once again, we found ourselves uprooting yet again for another job and moving from this beautiful place to somewhere I never dreamed of even visiting—Texas.

My Story

Trying to be positive about this move from an environmental oasis to a basically desert place was difficult. It was way too hot; the news reported "red ozone days" nearly every day of the summer. Our outdoor activities were moved to inside play dates. It was a tough transition for me as I loved being outdoors. Often I prayed for patience and guidance as I was being redefined again. We bought our first home and found a new church that welcomed us with open arms. I began to feel settled after a while and found Texans to be very gracious people. This was finally feeling like home as we adjusted to our new world. My husband loved his new job with Abbott

Laboratories and we were financially sound for the first time.

Our next mission was to try to help my mother who was having difficulty managing on her own back in Florida. Her health was in question and I was unable to care for her from a distance. After selling her rental properties, we convinced her to come live with us for a while. Our new house had an extra room that we had been planning to use for a third child—one that we now decorated and tried to make comfortable for my mom. As I was packing to leave for Florida to help my mother move, I noticed an odd bump on my husband's neck. Casually, I told him to get it checked as I was uncomfortable with it and thought it might be a lymph node that was swollen. It was probably just an infection we figured. It took me three days to pack up my mom and drive back to Texas. In that time, some dear friends lost their second baby to a rare brain cancer and my aunt lost her battle with colon cancer. Then my husband told me the lump on his neck had grown substantially. I needed to get home.

The doctor looked at the lump on my husband's neck and immediately sent him for x-rays. I was working in the garden when Doug came home from work unexpectedly. He asked me to drop what I was doing as he had some bad news. My heart sank. "The doctor says there is a tumor the size of my fist in my chest and they are pretty sure it is cancer." Oh my God, no, this can't be true…. Why?! How can it be as he runs eight-minute miles every day, mountain bikes and is the epitome of health? What do we do now? What do we tell the girls who are only ages two and four?

The next few weeks were quite a blur with doctor after doctor, test after test, surgeries, and telling our family and friends the horrifying news. We were completely overwhelmed and emotionally drained. As it turned out, Doug had stage IV small-cleaved B-cell follicular non-Hodgkin's lymphoma and they wanted to start chemotherapy right away. The oncologist could not believe that Doug had no symptoms up until this lump with the lymphoma so prevalent in his body. This disease, doctors told us, is incurable but very manageable. However, I don't think that was very comforting to any of us.

"Oh, and by the way, were you planning on having more

children? If so, you may want to think about banking sperm for future use as these drugs will leave your husband infertile," the doctor explained. "We will begin treatment in a few days."

Deciding your family's future in a few days is, to put it mildly, very difficult. We tried to find information about banking sperm, if the insurance covered it, how much it would cost, but it all seemed so trivial given that I may not have a husband or father to help raise our third child. So, we decided to forgo this option and just concentrate on beating this.

It was a long six months for us. We had the girls shave Doug's hair off before the chemo made it fall out to try to lessen the scariness of seeing Daddy change so much. My mom was there to help out when we thought we would be the ones helping her. She cared for the girls while we would be at the infusion room for hours on end. It was hard to keep things together for me—trying to make meals for Doug that he could or would eat, making other food for mom, the kids and I, or relying on the kindness of others to bring meals for us, trying to keep everything immaculate with little children in the house to prevent Doug from getting any secondary infections, keeping up the lawn because he could not be in the sun for long as one of the drugs made him ultra sensitive to the sun.

He was sick for several days after each chemo, which was usually administered on a Thursday or Friday to give him the weekend to recover. He would lie in bed all day, tired, drained, unable to play with the girls as he always did, and scared for his life—not the man I knew at all. Again, my life was being redefined for me. Now, I added the term "caregiver" to my list of titles. My husband is a brave man and never allowed this cancer to defeat him emotionally; he fought it tooth and nail until we got the news that he was in remission. Those were the most wonderful words to hear.

But, our lives had been totally changed by this experience. Not in a bad way necessarily—it is more of another gift, guiding us on our life path. The cancer made us realize how much we had been taking for granted, and we began living more full lives.

My mother decided to move back to Naples. The whole experience was very stressful on her and on our relationship. It was hard to let her go back but I understood and honestly needed the space to figure out my life again as well.

Doug quickly got stronger and stronger and things began to return to some normalcy. We hoped for a third child even though we knew the chances were slim. Doug was tested several months after his chemo had ended to see if there was any way we could conceive another child now that this cancer seemed behind us, but the tests confirmed that we would not be having any more children. We were okay with that. We had two beautiful daughters and were still together as a family; this was blessing enough.

It was now our five-year wedding anniversary. In celebration of both our marriage and Doug's new lease on life, we decided to take a trip to Hawaii without the children. His mom flew in from Michigan to help care for them while we were away. I also insisted that we prepare a will before leaving in case something happened. I was terrified of the thought that something terrible could happen, leaving them alone and wondering why we left. My rationalization was that it was prudent given the recent circumstances and life's way of throwing curve balls. Everything was in order when we left. We even discussed that third child again and decided it was not our decision but in God's hands at that point.

Hawaii was magical and romantic. We snorkeled, hiked, ate foods we couldn't pronounce and learned about island life. For those ten days, we were able to forget all the hell we had been through and enjoy one another in a way we had not been able to in a long while. Unfortunately, while hiking on the Napali cliffs in Kauai, I discovered I had a kidney stone, which severely limited my ability to hike as we had planned. We still managed to enjoy the rest of our vacation and returned home refreshed to our precious children whom we missed tremendously.

The kidney stone did not present a problem again for quite a while after we returned from Hawaii. One afternoon driving home from a play date, however, the pain became excruciating and I had to pull the car over. I began to feel faint but was able to get help from folks at a nearby boat shop, who called an ambulance and looked after the girls. In the emergency room, the nurse asked if

I could be pregnant and I explained our circumstances. She took a pregnancy test just as a precaution. As we expected, the test came back negative and I was sent for a CT scan to assess the stone. The technician not only found a stone but also a baby. We were pregnant! What a miracle. Our third daughter was born in December 2001 and thus our family was complete.

While I was pregnant with my third child, we became actively involved with the Leukemia & Lymphoma Society's Light the Night Walk to raise money for research, patient services and family assistance for those battling blood cancers. Our friends and family team has been the largest and one of the top fundraisers in our area since then, raising nearly $20,000 to date. Our church youth got involved in supporting us as well, and then one of the youth took ill and was diagnosed with Hodgkin's lymphoma.

Church members and neighbors began to tell us what an inspiration we were to them, asked us questions about cancer and detection, and some even shared their cancer experiences with us. By no means did we feel as though we should be anyone's inspiration; we were simply trying to survive and make it through our little tragedy the best we could. There were so many we had met and seen at the oncology center and at the Society events who had a great outlook despite overwhelming odds, grueling treatments and personal pain. Those people were truly inspirational as they never complained or whined about their circumstances but stood tall and walked with their feet firmly planted in the notion that this was not going to be their definition.

It was then Doug and I realized the gift we were given by this disease. It helped define both of us so we each could now be an empathetic, compassionate ear and voice to help others battle and win as we had. Again, our lives were being redefined. I prayed often for understanding as to what my purpose would be, how I was to use this curve ball, not just as a daughter, sister, wife and mother, but also as a part of the community. Beyond the Society's mission to find a cure and the impact that that would have on us, was there more I could or should be doing?

One early morning while it was still very dark outside, I woke up to a notion that it was time to start another Hands On Miami here in my new home of Texas. I got out of bed and went straight to the computer to research that possibility. Was there a similar organization already in existence in North Texas? If not, how would I go about this now, some eight years later and at my current life stage? Besides the scare of losing my husband and the girls' father, the cancer had rudely awakened me to the fact that I could or would at some point be the sole provider for my young daughters if my husband lost his battle. How would I make a living after being uprooted twice from any of the jobs I had held before becoming a mom and after being, basically, a housewife with no résumé now for well over five years?

This might be the answer. I could do this. I had the experience, the skills to create a new Cares organization here and, if I started it now, then perhaps by the time I needed it, I could draw a salary from it. Plus, it was my passion to help others, to get people involved in their community and work to better it together. It was idyllic and I loved it! It would allow me to bring my girls to volunteer with me while keeping me focused on the future and not lingering on what I cannot control with this disease. This work could help me connect to the community, help me build a résumé and eventually amount to a job that would give me the flexibility to be home for my daughters when they needed me. In addition, I could help show my daughters the difference they could make in the world and help them understand the blessings they have. I talked to my husband, who knew very well the work this entailed as he volunteered with me back in Miami quite often, and I got to work on building Greater Lewisville Cares, Inc.

As I got under way in filing for nonprofit status and began building a board of directors for Greater Lewisville Cares (GLC), my husband discovered new lumps that were eerily reminiscent of the ones he had found three years before. How could this be though? The oncologist told us we would have a good five to eight years before a recurrence of this cancer. Sure enough, it was back. This time we spent the first two years treating Doug with a monoclonal antibody treatment called Rituxan that had very little side effects. It was often used as a so-called "maintenance drug."

In the meantime, I continued to volunteer and grow and market GLC in the community, publishing the first calendar of service projects in May of 2004. It was a slow start and lots of work, but was very fulfilling for me personally; plus I had the added joy of including my daughters and husband in my work. Doug had also begun working with the Leukemia and Lymphoma Society's program called Team In Training. He decided to work toward competing in an upcoming Iron Man triathlon. He became the team's Honored Hero and spoke to participants about his story and what their efforts meant to so many. I helped him to get publicity in an effort to raise funds for this race as well as for my work.

My marketing, communications and public relations background came in handy in this new role in my life. I worked to get the girls' elementary school involved in the Society's mission with the Light the Night Walk and Pennies for Patients programs. This way the girls could be a part of helping their Dad and others in research for a cure. We were honest with our children about what was happening but we tried to remain positive on the outlook for the future. They did not need to be scared at such a young age about the possibility of losing their father, but still needed to understand the severity of the situation so they could ask questions and feel included.

Unfortunately, Doug's cancer grew worse as he got closer to the Iron Man race to be held in Utah. Serendipitously, he injured his hip while training, which ultimately forced him to postpone the race and begin a more systemic, aggressive cancer treatment once again. He had so hoped to be able to accomplish his goal of an Iron Man before succumbing to the disease again. But, God's will seemed to be telling us that treatment was where our focus should be. For the next six months or so, Doug endured a new chemo regimen that we hoped would give him another remission and buy us more time together as a family.

Our spirits were bruised but not so much so that we could not see the light at the end of the tunnel. We just hunkered down into a routine that had become unfortunately fairly routine, relying again on friends to help juggle our children's schedules and trying to keep everything as "normal" as possible. Our daughters were now ages nine, seven and three. The Leukemia and Lymphoma Society asked us to join the Light the Night Walk committee for Denton, Texas, and Doug continued to inspire athletes going the extra mile with Team In Training. Our motives here were as much selfish as selfless in that we hoped our efforts in raising money for the Society would help bring a cure for us and for all those we had come to know and love. People looked to us for inspiration, although we did not feel that role was ours to claim as we were simply trying to survive the best way we could.

To date, Greater Lewisville Cares (GLC) has done well, too, with over 250 members, several teams from local churches and organizations, and various companies contacting us to help provide opportunities for their employees to reach out to the community. Local social service agencies have come to rely on GLC when they need help. Our volunteers have logged well over 2,500 hours of service in the two years we have been in business mentoring children and teen moms, delivering meals to the elderly, building wheelchair ramps, working with those in need at local food pantries and soup kitchens, aiding victims of natural disasters, and picking up trash in our neighborhoods, among many others.

Friends often comment, "I don't know how you do it all!" The thing is, this is my therapy. Through volunteering, I can help with problems that are fixable such as making sure a child has help with homework or an elderly person gets their one meal a day or the pantry is manned and stocked. What I cannot control is a disease that has infiltrated my life and turned it virtually upside down. So many of the ills of our community are very fixable—a matter of the "haves" sharing with the "have-nots," or existing resources and assistance programs being made more available to those they are meant to help.

My hope is to educate those of us who are financially able and willing, who have skills and resources available to lend a hand—not necessarily a handout—to aid those beaten down by a fallible system. To give hope to kids caught in a cycle of poverty or abuse, so they can live the same dream—the American dream—of having a good life, providing for their families and being a viable part of a caring community. No one in this rich country should have to go without if this is not their choice and if they are willing to work hard. No one. Not one child, not one senior, not one teen, not one battered woman—no one.

This is not impossible if we work together. I have seen us jump to action to aid hurricane victims, producing warehouses filled with furniture, clothing, toys, food, and more at a moment's notice, or pouring millions of dollars into aid for those affected in the tsunami disaster. Doing this, for me as a Christian, is not only the right thing to do, it is what God commands us to do. I believe this is my definition, this is my calling among being a mother, daughter, wife, sister, friend—ultimately, I am a child of God just like my neighbor, the check-out person at the grocery store, the man suffering in the infusion room just a few chairs from my husband. We all have a story, we all have dreams, and we all try to live the best we can with the cards life has dealt us. As Winston Churchill said, "We make a living by what we get, but we make a life by what we give."

In Conclusion

As change is an inevitable part of life, learning to embrace it and find comfort in our faith to see us through it will give us the ability to look to the future with joy rather than becoming lost in the circumstances of the present. We can choose to be defined by the changes that come our way during our lives, or we can take those changes and decide how to use them to create a definition for ourselves that offers hope, faith, courage, growth, understanding and compassion in whatever circumstance we are faced with. I hope my story, which is not unlike many, will somehow help you to discover the joy of this journey called life and embrace the thrill of the roller coaster rides that are an inherent part of the adventure.

Questions to Ponder

1. Is this changing moment a defining one or just a temporary one? Can I see past it to the next phase of my life or see an end

where things will return to normal?

2. How can I use this change to define or redefine myself in the future?

3. Has this change been forced upon me or something I chose for myself? Why?

4. Am I at a life-altering place in my life? If so, how do I feel about myself and where I am at the time this change happened to me? Is this where I want to be?

5. Is this change a chronic or life-threatening illness? Do I want this disease to define me or will I define who I will be despite this disease?

6. Have I set goals for my life and amended them as my life has evolved?

A Closing Thought From Ben and Ken

Sometimes change enters our lives in profoundly difficult ways. The loss of a parent, a spouse's illness, career changes coupled with moving everything across the country and back, all result in painful life changes. Stacey has seen them all, yet she has found ways to pull something positive from the darkest events. Her deep faith and her indomitable spirit have driven her to seek the good in whatever tragedy she's faced.

Likewise, the longer you live, the more certain crisis or tragedy will touch your life. Our bonus years should not be defined by the difficulties or changes that come our way. Instead, we should find the grace to respond to these inevitable situations without letting them destroy us in the process.

Stacey has found ways to enrich the lives of those around her. She has become one who serves the needs of others and in doing so has found strength for her own life. You, too, can find strength in reaching out to others in your church, synagogue, or community volunteer program. In serving others it is possible to find healing for yourself. What a great way to spend some of your bonus years.

SPREADING THE SEEDS OF OPPORTUNITY
Mona Parish

... A farmer went out to sow his seed. As he was scattering the seed, some fell along the path, and the birds came and ate it up. Some fell on rocky places, where it did not have much soil. It sprang up quickly, because the soil was shallow. But when the sun came up, the plants were scorched, and they withered because they had no root. Other seed fell among thorns, which grew up and choked the plants. Still other seed fell on good soil, where it produced a crop—a hundred, sixty or thirty times what was sown.

Matthew 13:3-8

Many seeds of change are planted in every person's life. For some, life may change abruptly, with an uprooting from one place or situation, or with a crisis circumstance that must be met by a rearrangement of priorities or a shedding of one set of responsibilities for another. But for some of us, the seeds of change take root and grow over time. Small changes occur—changes that are not remarkable in themselves, but which reveal themselves to be astonishing and miraculous when one compares the mature flower with the seed from which it sprang.

The seed that grew into my current position as executive director of Care Net Pregnancy Center of Northwest Houston was planted many years ago, I am sure, but I remember becoming aware of that seed at about the age of 40. At that time I was a full time homemaker with two teen-aged children. I had earned a degree in sociology from Stephen F. Austin State University in 1974, and had worked in banking for about six years before resigning to begin raising a family. When my youngest was in preschool, I went back to school myself to get a teaching credential, and taught elementary school for about five years before a family move to Houston from the San Antonio area caused me to decide to once again stay home as a full time mom. In addition to family responsibilities, my time was taken up with volunteering at the children's schools—PTO and Band Boosters, Moms in Prayer and office work.

Not far from the neighborhood where I lived was a suburban medical center. At the time of the seed planting, somewhere in one of the office buildings there was an abortion provider. When I drove past the medical center I would see people standing outside holding signs about killing babies, shouting at women, planting crosses in the ground to signify the death of babies in the clinic. The signs that they carried and the slogans they shouted were condemnatory of both the abortion provider and of the women who chose to patronize the clinic to receive abortion services.

In all of the times that I drove by, I never saw a sign of compassion for the women who were making the difficult choice to end the life of a child. I hated that. I do not believe that women coldly and cruelly murder their babies. My heart went out, not only to the babies, but to the women who found themselves in a situation where they felt they had to make this choice. What must they be feeling as they came to the doctor's office or clinic—surely some sadness at the loss, surely some confusion over their choice. And to be met by condemnation and shouts of derision would not soften their hearts but harden them against those people and what they represented. Rather than making it easier to make the choice that the protesters desired, the judgment and condemnation of the protesters made it easier to continue with the plan, feeling justified in what they were doing, feeling the righteousness of a martyr.

Why, I thought, could those who carried signs and shouted not just offer help or a listening ear to women coming into the clinic? Were those protesters willing to offer practical help to someone who really wanted to carry her baby but felt constrained by very real financial considerations? Were they willing to support, both financially and emotionally, just one young woman during the term of her pregnancy so that she could then go on to school or her career? Were they willing to intervene in an abusive relationship? In short, was anyone willing to provide support rather than condemnation?

The Bible tells a story of a woman who was caught in the act of adultery and brought to Jesus to receive his judgment. Rather than condemn the woman, Jesus challenged those who had dragged her before them. Was there one of them who had not sinned in some way? If so, Jesus invited that person to cast the first stone. All of the accusers walked away, knowing that they were also standing under condemnation for whatever sin was in their lives.

Was Jesus' example of love and forgiveness toward the woman caught in adultery possibly what was called for in this situation? I wasn't ready yet to respond, but a seed was planted in my mind and in my heart.

I knew at that point that there had to be another way to approach the problem of unwanted pregnancies, but I didn't know how to respond as an individual, and I wasn't aware of an organization that offered the help I thought was necessary. I was wary of becoming involved with a "pro-life" movement that offered only condemnation with no real answers for women. I knew I did not want to be involved in any way with that group of people who stood outside of clinics shouting. God allowed me to live for a while with those feelings of self-righteousness before bringing before me an opportunity to transform my condemnation of the protesters into positive action. At church one Sunday I saw a brochure offering information about volunteering at a crisis pregnancy center. At the time I had no knowledge of what was involved, but I picked up the brochure, thinking I would like to know more about what services were offered to women in a crisis pregnancy. The brochure said that the center offered free pregnancy testing and peer counseling. It also talked about emotional and practical support through pregnancy. I remember feeling that maybe this was the avenue that *someone* could use to make a real difference with women facing unplanned or crisis pregnancies. But I was also afraid that the pregnancy center was a front, and that it was really a support center for those people I felt did so much harm in the name of loving life. I squirreled away the brochure, not wanting to become a part of the controversy over abortion, but knowing that lives were more likely to be changed by the kinds of services they said they offered than by shouting. The seed was being watered.

I did not take action right away, but after seeing the brochure several more times over the course of the next few months, I finally made the call to ask about volunteering at the pregnancy center. Training for new volunteers was to begin within the next month. I decided to at least attend the training and learn more about the ministry. I could decide later whether or not to actually become a volunteer based on what I learned there. At the very least I would be able to pat myself on the back that I had thought about trying to make a difference.

The first night of volunteer training, I remember the director saying, "We are the kinder, gentler side of pro-life." That resonated with me as the kind of response I had been looking for. There was a realization in this organization that the pro-life movement cannot save the lives of babies without loving the mothers, too. The path to changing women's hearts lay in caring for them practically, emotionally and spiritually. I learned more about the services offered, and discovered that many who worked or volunteered at the center had been touched in some way by their own crisis pregnancy or abortion, or that of a family member. Because of the experiences and witness of those volunteers, there was no temptation to condemn, for many of these people had stood exactly where the young women who came to the center for help were standing. That realization relaxed my thinking about the center and its role in the lives of women—and families—affected by an unplanned or unwanted pregnancy. It seemed I had found a place that was responding in the way that I thought we should respond to people in need. I completed the training and became a volunteer peer counselor for what was then Northwest Pregnancy Center in Houston, Texas.

My life changed, not in response to a big decision and conscious change of direction, but as a result of responding to circumstances that were placed before me. I believe that God knew what he was doing as he led me little by little to do the things he was preparing for me. Had he even intimated to me that I would be the executive director within 10 years, I would have run, quickly, in another—any other—direction. So how does one make that change from volunteer to executive director in the least scary way possible? Step by very small step! As a volunteer, I gave four hours a week to the center. My job was to visit with young women who came to the center for a free pregnancy test. I could find out what their needs were—materially, emotionally and spiritually.

At the center we offered maternity clothing and baby items such as diapers and equipment. Sometimes just knowing that those things were available to fall back on if needed gave women the encouragement they needed. At other times clients needed to be referred to social service agencies that could help with material needs. If we were not able to provide specific help at the center, most of the time we could find help through another agency or organization. Many times, though, just a supporting ear was what was needed. In my life, this was the answer for a place to make a difference. I volunteered weekly at the center for several years, never thinking that my involvement would move beyond those four hours a week.

Then in 2001, when I was 47 years old, one of the employees was involved in an accident that left her unable to work for a period of time. When it became apparent that she needed more time to recuperate, and also that her job at the center could not be left unattended any longer, I asked the executive director if I could temporarily step into that position just to allow the injured employee the time she needed to be well enough to return to the job. A full time permanent position was not a consideration—I was happy with my life the way it was, and the other employee would be returning in a matter of a few months, if not a few weeks. However, when it became apparent that the person who had held the job would not return, I was offered the position of client services director.

Accepting this position put me in charge of providing services to clients by training, scheduling and overseeing volunteers. I also had a chance to work with clients who needed more specific resources than the volunteers were prepared to provide—to go a little deeper in meeting their needs. In addition to the position as client services director, I was named Mercy Project director. The Mercy Project is the educational outreach of the pregnancy center. We offer classes in the areas of health, pregnancy and baby care, life applications, and work skills. Our purpose is not only to prepare the women and men we serve to be good parents, but to provide them with useful information such as budgeting and job related skills. This was not the direction I had thought my life would take, but at this point moving into a full time position seemed like the next logical step in my search to make a difference.

I loved my new job. I still got to work with clients and I got to be at the center full time. It was a whole new world. As a volunteer I saw women as they came into the Center for the first time. There was some follow-up, but if a client returned to the center to take classes or to receive assistance at a time when I was not there, I was largely unaware of it. As client services and Mercy Project director, I saw clients come and go many times and was able to develop longer term relationships with them. I knew what classes they were taking and was able to be instrumental in shaping those classes to meet needs. I knew their long term goals and plans on a deeper level and could have some input in making some of those plans come to fruition. It was even more of where I longed to be in response to women in need.

In January of 2004, another employee was added at the center. Nanda Kirkpatrick took over as Mercy Project director and I retained the job of client services director, which allowed both jobs to grow in order to better serve clients. In October of the same year, after I had been on staff for about three years, the long-time executive director of the center resigned to move out of state with her family.

At that time, the center was in a financial crisis and could not afford to replace the director. Nanda and I went to the board of directors and offered to maintain our current salaries, and to split up the duties previously covered by the executive director. We offered to do this for the period of a year, knowing that we would be putting in lots of extra hours and that we couldn't commit to that schedule for the long term. Making that commitment for a year would hopefully allow the center to recover financially to be able to hire someone to fill the position of executive director. However, the financial condition of the center was such that no one on the board, and certainly neither of the key employees, would have given any guarantee that the center would even be in existence by the time a year had passed. Knowing that we might be presiding over the demise of the ministry, I became center director and Nanda became associate director. I was 50 years old.

Less than two years later, I am serving as the executive director of a financially viable ministry. I work with a phenomenal team of women and men, both staff and volunteers. Nanda still serves as associate director and is a vital part of the day to day management of the center. There has been a huge learning curve—I went from ministering to women by being a friend, to dealing with issues like lease renewal, insurance, technology issues and building maintenance. However, God has been faithful to provide needed assistance in those areas where I lack expertise, and the journey has certainly been exciting. I am still able to interact with clients; each of the staff members serves as a peer counselor at least one hour a week. However, the focus of my personal ministry has shifted to providing for staff and volunteer needs to enable them to minister directly to clients.

Making the transition was a step by step process. I loved counseling with clients when I began as a volunteer. When I moved into a staff position, I missed the intense day to day contact with clients, but came to realize that my calling at that point was to provide for the needs of the volunteers so that they were free to deal directly with clients. I was able to serve even more clients by ministering to the volunteers. In the same way, when I moved into the executive director position, I realized that my job became ministering to our staff so that the staff would be able to minister to the volunteers so that they, in turn, could minister to the clients. I have a new appreciation for the difficult issues dealt with at the leadership level; learning to handle the business concerns of the ministry and dealing with the political realities of the non-profit world has been an interesting excursion into a field I could not have anticipated for my life. The job I do now would have seemed so overwhelming when I first made the call to attend volunteer training. But by following the baby steps as they were set before me, I have learned much and grown into new responsibilities and joys.

What has it meant to change my life from homemaker and volunteer to full time career ministry after the age of 40? I count many blessings. My husband and I are empty nesters, and we have the flexibility to spend time at our jobs and to enjoy each other during our time off. I am so awed that I have the opportunity to serve in new ways and to learn skills in new areas as I grow older. At a time of life when many are winding down their work lives, I feel like my career is vital and exciting and meaningful. My dream of making a difference in the lives of women faced with an agonizing choice has become a reality in a bigger way than I would have thought possible. At a time when many of my peers are questioning their life's work and wondering if their most important contributions are in the past, I can honestly say that there is more to learn, more to do, more to give.

Although the changes in my life came in baby steps, I can look back and see a clear path from where I began to where I am. As I look at the story of how my life has changed after 40, it is clear that those changes have been rooted in God's activity in my life. It is not necessarily a reflection of my faith, which sometimes falters and is certainly imperfect, but is instead a reflection of God's faithfulness and unmerited grace. I serve in full time Christian ministry to women, men and families facing a crisis or unplanned pregnancy. I consider the opportunity of service as a gift from God. It is he who placed the baby steps before me and gave me the courage to take each one.

Questions:

1. Is there an area where you feel there is an injustice or a need that is not being met?

2. Is there an area where you feel that SOMEONE should step in and do something? Is there a baby step you can make to help meet the need or challenge the injustice?

3. What organizations or institutions are already in place that are attempting to meet the need? Even if they are not perfect, is there a way that you can begin serving within an existing framework rather than starting from scratch?

A Closing Thought From Ben and Ken

People who are angry and judgmental use so much of their energy that it's difficult for them to be part of the solution. Mona rejected that path and instead made the decision to be a healing force.

How you spend your bonus years is largely dependent upon how you respond to others. Is there a clinched fist or an open hand? Do you condemn or embrace? Mona is choosing to use her bonus years helping others.

Read again Mona's questions at the end of her chapter and see if they make you think of some way to reach out in a world that needs caring. There are an unbelievable number of charities, non-profit centers, homeless shelters, and the like where you can use your bonus years to touch the lives of others.

Remember the great quote by Sir Winston Churchill, "We make a living by what we get; we make a life by what we give."

Chapter 8

CLEARED FOR A VISUAL APPROACH
Captain Ken Arthur

What you are is more basic than what you do.
—Dr. John Claypool

Over my career as an airline captain, I've heard literally hundreds of airport tower controllers say, "You're cleared for a visual approach." To a pilot, those few words are both liberating and constraining.

From takeoff to landing, commercial flights are usually under Air Traffic Control (ATC) supervision. Other than in emergency situations, we're told where to taxi, when to takeoff, what direction to go, what altitude to maintain, when to descend or climb, even what airspeed to fly.

That close supervision is usually maintained all the way to landing, especially when the weather is bad. When there is low visibility such as fog, rain, or clouds near the airport, controllers give vectors or directions for pilots to follow. Even though the pilots perhaps can't see any ground references, the controller's vectors will end at an instrument approach from which the pilot will carefully fly specific procedures, descend and land the aircraft safely. When flying in this kind of weather, the pilot may not see the runway until just a few feet above the ground. Obviously, when the visibility is this low, pilots cannot see other aircraft so separation must be provided by ATC. Planes must be kept farther apart. This is why there are often delays when the weather is marginal. For safety's sake, there just can't be as many aircraft near the airport at the same time.

However, on days when the weather is good and visibility is unrestricted, pilots are responsible to see and avoid other aircraft. Around major airports with multiple runways, there can be planes coming from many directions at once. ATC will keep them separated and will inform pilots of other aircraft who are possible conflicts. Controllers are very good at this, and conflicts are extremely rare. The controllers are compelled to continually update each pilot to all known traffic.

Ultimately, however, even with ATC and electronic assistance, the pilots in the planes are responsible to "see and avoid" other aircraft. That responsibility ensures pilots are diligently searching for possible conflicts in their flight path. It also means they are always aware of their position in relation to the airport.

Because there are more aircraft in the vicinity of a major airport, a controller might be calling out traffic continuously—even on a clear day—to planes that are not a potential conflict.

However, once a pilot can see the airport and the runway he will land upon, he can expedite the flight by informing the tower of that fact. Usually this will result in the tower responding, "You're cleared for a visual approach."

Visual approach means the pilot is now free to maneuver the aircraft in any way he or she wants in order to land at the destination runway. There will be no further vectors or directions from the tower to assist the pilots, and there will be no further warnings about other aircraft or conflicts. With a visual approach, the pilot can now do anything he or she wants to do. However, the tower is released from responsibility for the flight.

From the flight deck, the pilots are looking ahead to the spot they want to land. Their job has been to bring their passengers hundreds, perhaps thousands, of miles to safely reach this place. They are totally responsible for reaching their destination.

It's been my experience that life is often like a visual approach. We're given directions that others feel will help us. We listen to advice from parents, teachers, friends, educators, and spiritual leaders, but in the end, we're responsible for reaching our own life goals. We still have to find our own way. That means learning everything possible from those around us without giving up our own ideas and values.

This isn't just a hypothetical concept for me. I spent the first 27 years of my life pursuing a career that wasn't really what I wanted to do. It was my expected path.

From my teenage years, faith was an important part of my experience. Church activities were the central focus of my week. Our church youth choir made two concert tours over a large part of the United States and four provinces of Canada. In high school, I became the president of a non-denominational Christian group on my high school campus.

Soon, opportunities to speak to different church youth groups and congregations developed.

Before long, people started expecting me to become a preacher. The expectations of others started affecting the way I saw myself. It didn't take too long before I began to accept their belief that the ministry was my path. Once I became known as a "future preacher," the snowball started rolling downhill, gaining mass and speed. There was no way to see anything else as my destiny.

After my wife Mary and I earned our undergraduate college degrees, I entered seminary and completed a three year long master's degree. Following graduate school, we moved to central Texas where I had been hired as a college campus minister for two junior colleges. No formal college ministry had been done on these campuses in several years so it was an opportunity to begin something completely new.

This challenge was exciting and I had both the enthusiasm and zeal to make things happen. Soon, 80 hour work weeks began showing results. There were meetings almost every night, numerous dormitory Bible studies, weekly conferences with each of my student leadership, community ministries to lead, and relationships to cultivate with the local pastors and church staffs. Within 18 months, there were several hundred students involved in some aspect of the campus ministry. By any standard, the ministry was successful. It was growing and our students were maturing spiritually as they became actively involved in Bible studies and community mission projects.

Despite the accomplishments, I was not happy. The long days were draining and the self-induced pressure to do more was wearing me down. Plus, I was slowly realizing my drive and motivation to see the ministry grow was at least partially personal. I wanted others to know that *I* had done this great thing of beginning and growing this wonderful ministry. As a minister, I honestly wanted to give God the credit for the work, and did so publicly. It was the inner dialog where I wasn't being honest.

As often happens in life, an unexpected misfortune changed the course of my snowball's path. I unwisely had a conflict with a very senior leader in our denomination. Even though it was resolved, I knew realistically my career was going to be affected.

This harsh realization made me ponder where I was heading with my life. It seemed that all I had worked for was now lost.

By now, Mary and I had a baby girl named Kristi. We had a mortgage on our small home. What could I possibly do? I was a minister. That's what I did. That was all I knew.

Or was it?

Many years before, I was taught by a remarkable high school teacher who made a huge impact on my life. He was a retired naval aviator who had become a trigonometry teacher. He spoke to his classes about flying and made it seem so amazing. Often after class I would talk with him about being a pilot. He encouraged me to follow my dreams.

Flying had always held a deep fascination for me. While in seminary, I earned a private pilot's license. I could only do this because one friend named Gary Warden owned a plane he let me fly for very little money. Another friend, Robert Whitley, was a certified flight instructor who taught me to fly for free.

Because of the encouragement and help of these three men — my high school trig teacher, Gary Warden, and Robert Whitley — I would years later consider a new path for my life.

After my problems with the religious denomination leader, I

was certain I needed to consider that different path. The decision I made seems radical even all these years later. I visited an Air Force recruiter to find out about pilot training. Countless written forms, examinations, interviews, and medical tests followed. It took almost a year before I received the news I had been accepted to Air Force Undergraduate Pilot Training (UPT).

What a switch in careers! From minister to Air Force pilot. My wife and I knew somehow it was the right thing to do and we were excited about the future.

After commissioning as a second lieutenant, I entered UPT. Even the beginning of training had its excitement. The morning before I started, my wife gave birth to our son Kevin.

The year of pilot training was easily the most challenging time of my life, but I loved it. Each day consisted of 12 hours in classes and flying followed by four hours studying each night. Every weekend was the same—family or church time until noon and then study the rest of the day.

Over the years I've come to believe that no experience or training is ever a waste of time. Eventually, you will be in a situation that calls for a skill or some knowledge you picked up perhaps years before.

To illustrate my belief, during UPT I started preaching at a small country church. This was a difficult thing to do because of the very little amount of free hours I had to spare. After a short time, they asked me to become their pastor. Somehow, the time to prepare sermons worked into the day. This seemed to be a confirmation that perhaps my seminary years had not been a waste of time. I could follow my dream to fly and still minister.

After earning my silver Air Force pilot's wings, I began training as an instructor pilot (IP). A three year tour at the same UPT base followed and I continued pastoring the little country church on Sundays.

Those three years as an IP passed quickly and it was time to receive my next assignment. The little country church found a new minister and that particular chapter of my life was complete.

After my tour as an IP, my next assignment was to Europe to fly the F-111 stationed at Royal Air Force Base Lakenheath, England. My wife and I prepared for a major move with Kristi, now seven, and Kevin who was five. We were headed to England for what ended up being just short of four years. Another adventure.

The F-111 was an amazing jet. Our mission was to fly at very low altitudes at unbelievable speeds to destroy high priority enemy targets. Our main protection came from being below most radars and being faster than the enemy's jets. This kind of flying was dangerous and demanding but was a challenge every pilot who flew the F-111 loved. To become "mission ready" took almost an additional year of training. As a mission ready F-111 pilot, I was routinely flying as low as 200 feet above the ground at more than 500 miles per hour.

As an additional duty, I was the chief of current operations for the 48th Tactical Fighter Wing at RAF Lakenheath, England. In this role, I was responsible for scheduling and allocating flight operations for the wing. The job required developing the skill of keeping a myriad of details straight at all times. It was challenging work, but these learned skills would prove to be crucial to success in later life. Another benefit of this difficult job was the quality of individuals with whom I worked, many of whom I've stayed close to through the years.

Those years in England went by quickly and we came to another crossroads. My commitment to the Air Force was almost complete and Mary and I had to decide whether to stay in the military or return to civilian life.

One factor to consider was that the major airlines were growing and hiring. No one knew how long that would last.

Once again, we decided I would change careers. This was as uncomfortable a move as was leaving the ministry. We were leaving a steady paycheck and a "company" that would never go bankrupt. We were entering an industry known for its turmoil and financial uncertainties. Still somehow we knew it was the right thing to do.

Just like with joining the Air Force, becoming an airline pilot involved examinations, interviews, flight simulator check rides, and a medical exam tougher and more thorough than any I had ever had in my life.

Finally, I received the great news of being hired by my first choice in airlines. Our family moved back to our home state of Texas and was soon settled into the civilian world of commercial aviation. These were the halcyon days of growth for the airline industry with new aircraft being bought and a boom in hiring.

Our children were now 12 and nine. They had lived a significant part of their lives in England and traveled all over Europe. Coming back to the United States was a cultural shock to them, but they adapted quickly.

Flying in the civilian world was significantly different from the military, but I enjoyed this new career. Never again would I know the excitement of flying a fighter, of feeling the power of an afterburner kick the jet faster than the speed of sound. I missed the precision of formation flying ... of being three feet away from another jet at 500 miles per hour.

There were new joys, however, to be discovered in aviation. For example, I found a huge enjoyment in accepting the responsibility of flying a jet airliner full of passengers. I loved the challenge of making a smooth landing ... after all, that's what most passengers remember about a flight.

In commercial aviation, regardless of how much flight time pilots have, they inevitably begin as flight engineers or first officers (co-pilots). My career followed that expected path. Eventually, however, my seniority permitted me to upgrade and fly as captain.

For a pilot, there is no higher place to be than captain, flying in the left seat for a major airline. I had reached the pinnacle of my profession.

In 2000, I was selected to work in the airline as a check airman. My experience years before as an Air Force Instructor Pilot was a definite factor in being selected as a check airman. In this role, I gave training and evaluations to other pilots. For me, it was the best job in the company. Some of the brightest pilots I'd ever known were in the cadre of check airmen. It was my ultimate job, and one I looked forward to doing until I would retire in 2012. At least that was my plan until September 11, 2001. Suddenly, our airline, like most, was stagnant and even shrinking. The check airman job evaporated, and

I was back flying as a line captain. Worse, it was not the same job I had left just over a year before.

September 11 obviously had a profound effect on the airline industry. For the traveling public, flying became a much more inconvenient process. For flight crews, it had a deeper impact. Our way of operating changed dramatically. Our cockpits became fortresses. Procedures changed sometimes daily as we sought ways to be proactive to the possibility of a changing terrorism threat.

I can honestly say I never felt uncomfortable flying, even after September 11. Unfortunately, there were other factors that began to invade our industry. Rising fuel costs drastically affected the bottom line for all airlines. Instead of great profits, they were now swimming in red ink. Our airline laid off thousands of employees in an effort to stay out of bankruptcy. Every employee group in the company made substantial sacrifices in pay, benefits, and work rules to help. With fewer pilots left, I was a reserve pilot. In this role, I never knew when I would fly. The schedulers would call and I'd have to leave for up to four days on as little as an hour's notice. We were always flying the maximum days, but had no control over our lives. We couldn't plan any event because there was no real stability. Even some of our "days off" could be changed around by the schedulers.

My profession had become a job. As much as I loved the company and flying, I knew this wasn't what I wanted to do the rest of my working career. I made the difficult decision to start a fourth career.

As you can imagine, some people questioned my decision. One place where that didn't happen was in our company flight operations. I talked with many other pilots and only one thought I was making a mistake. All the others said they wished they had the courage or financial ability to make the change.

I always loved, and will always love, the thrill of flying. In the past 30 years, I've flown everything from small single engine airplanes to multiengine jet airliners and Air Force fighters. Even with 10,000 flight hours, the adventure and satisfaction of flying an airplane has never gotten old for me. It wasn't flying or the company—it was the job that had lost its luster.

Of course, leaving the airline was difficult for other reasons. I knew I wouldn't find a job approaching the salary I was making after more than 17 years as a commercial pilot and captain. However, both of my children had already completed their undergraduate degrees from a great university and were self sufficient. That major financial responsibility was behind us, which made the transition easier.

I'm now involved with an industry where I draw upon the experience I had in the Air Force. Those years of scheduling and logistics in a fighter wing fit perfectly to an industry where one needs to orchestrate complex and ever-changing events.

Every change Mary and I have faced in our 36 years of marriage has made us accept some basic "truths" that work for us:

1. When considering any major change, you have to do your homework. Consider as many factors as you can. Find out as many pros and cons for the opportunity as possible. Think about the *what ifs*, but don't allow yourself to become so involved with them that you don't do anything. It's been our experience that ultimately you have to trust your instincts. Do what you feel in your heart is the right thing to do. If you've done your research and found out as much as possible about the choice you're making, you can trust your gut level instinct.

2. Remember that in the final analysis there is no such thing as a self-made man or woman. We all stand on the shoulders of everyone who has helped form us and our abilities. I could list over a hundred people who have in one way or another helped make me who I am today. Don't be afraid to ask advice from people you trust—but remember only you can decide ultimately what is best.

3. Don't think that the job you're doing right now will have no impact on your future. This is a trap many young people fall into right after college when they're in their first "real" job. It's easy to do that even later in life. My seminary degree seemed totally useless in the Air Force, but it opened a door to do ministry. My instructor pilot time in the Air Force helped me be hired years later as a check airman for my airline. My Air Force work as a scheduler and logistics manager was the key to the job I found after the airline.

In each of these cases, I never imagined that years later what I was doing would open another door. Keep this in mind when you feel your present circumstance is a "dead-end" job.

4. Keep a "rainy day" fund or savings account going. Sometimes it takes a while to find the next career opportunity.

5. If you decide to change career directions in your life, consider the old adage, "It's easier to find a new job while you're still working." I found that to be true. (See number 4 above.)

6. This is the most important truth I've found: If there is someone significant to you, a wife or husband, you can't leave them out of the decision making process. My wife Mary has been an amazing partner throughout the 36 years we've been married. Her advice and insight have always been a key factor in our decision process, and not just about career changes. This is true despite the fact that I got her to marry me under "false pretenses." As a starry eyed 18-year-old, she thought she was marrying a future preacher. We struggled together to both get our undergraduate degrees. She supported me when I was in graduate school. Afterward, she was the perfect minister's wife. Then we jointly decided to consider a radical change. She became an Air Force officer's spouse with all the responsibilities that accompanied my positions. Later, she adapted again to civilian life. Finally, she supported us again until I established my latest career. Most important of all, she's never lost her own identity. Mary has grown and flourished in her career, both professionally and educationally. Having a wife like Mary is a blessing beyond description. You've probably already met her in this book.

Consider one last thought. Sometimes we get our sense of self worth from our job. That concept can leave you feeling insignificant if your job or salary or prestige doesn't move in what most people consider an upward direction. Below the title to this chapter is a quote from Dr. John Claypool. "What you are is more basic than what you do." I heard Dr. Claypool make that statement almost 30 years ago while attending a chapel service. Like so many ideas this great pastor, author, and speaker communicated, the true profound depth of his statement wasn't immediately obvious to me. Yet later, as I considered his comment, I experienced a feeling of excitement that continues to this day. Our importance to God, our basic being, is not dependent upon what we *do*. It comes just from the fact that we *are*. We don't earn our worth from where we are on the corporate ladder.

For my family and me, career decisions have developed into a simple but tough mantra: Never be afraid to consider a new opportunity. As adults, we have the unique ability to make decisions that affect us personally. New career opportunities abound that can stimulate and challenge you. You may have to be willing to learn new skills, take classes, study hard, maybe even take an initial pay cut in order to fulfill a dream. Those sacrifices may end up being insignificant compared to the satisfaction of conquering your fears and attaining what may have been a life-long goal. Your bonus years might well be your best years.

You're cleared for a visual approach with your destiny. Most of all remember, life is short—enjoy every day of it.

A Closing Thought From Ben

When a person's self worth is completely tied to their job title or pay structure, it can be a struggle when those things are altered. Also, changing careers can be a frightening and difficult decision for anyone. As a result, some people stay in their comfort zone even though they are unhappy. They may not enjoy their work, and yet won't change because it's familiar and secure. "Better the devil you know" would be their motto.

For Ken and his family, the courage to move into new and exciting careers was a way to continue growing. They recognized that being willing to take risks can be absolutely crucial to reaching your highest potential. More importantly, they recognized that nothing is ever wasted. Even experience you receive in a less than perfect job can be exactly what you need years later to excel in a great job.

We are all responsible for our own actions and decisions. The concept of a "visual approach" giving us the freedom to maneuver our plans as we see fit can be a liberating thought. Make your plans, do your research, get the best advice you can find, and move ahead to accomplish your highest dreams. What better way to spend some of your bonus years?

Chapter 9

"WITH YOUR NEXT HUSBAND"
Gay Bearden

Somehow he knew. He always knew that he wouldn't live that long. He always used to say to me "…with your next husband…" It was his way of preparing me for life without him.

I grew up in West Texas. Born in a small town outside of Lubbock, I was the younger of two girls born to a mother who was a voice teacher of some renown in the area and a salesman father. We always knew a lot of love and my childhood was typical of the idyllic 1950s. I went to college at West Texas State University in Canyon, Texas, and became a history major. What does one do with a major in history? I became a teacher.

I have always loved history and government and teaching was a logical extension of that love. In 1975, I got involved with law-related education and found a new love—law. Rather than go to law school, I decided to share my love through teaching students about the law. Not the droll everyday aspects of law, but the pure law as handed down by our founding fathers and Supreme Court cases. It became my passion to instill my new-found love of law in my students, and that passion continues today.

In 1978, I moved to Dallas and taught Texas history and U.S. history at a middle school. There, I met an art teacher named Bob Bearden. From the beginning, I knew I was attracted to him, but I wouldn't allow myself to get involved with him because he was not only a teacher, but divorced with custody of his two small daughters. I could not see myself as an instant mother. For the three years I taught there, we were just friends and I would not allow it to go any further. In 1981, I was offered a position leading the law program in the Dallas schools. Since I knew I was leaving, I decided to take a chance and see him. That was all it took. I knew I was hopelessly in love with him from that moment on. Somehow, he was the man I had been looking for all my life.

We married in November of 1981. He had custody of his twin daughters, Hayden and Mecca, who were just four when we married. I raised them and have always loved them as my own. Our daughter Rachel was born in 1983.

Bob was a true "renaissance man." He was the most intelligent, talented and yet complicated man I have ever known. There was nothing he couldn't do. He was a gourmet chef and an accomplished artist; he could fix anything from rebuilding an engine to constructing a house. His broad knowledge of so many, many things continually amazed me. Bob, always the teacher, insisted that I learn the "how-to" of all the things we worked on together. I think this was his way of preparing me to be alone.

Bob was always an active person. He never just sat. He always had a project of some sort going. During the summer of 2001, his latest project was to build a shed roof over the barbecue and rework the stairs on our deck. He worked long hours outside in the heat and started to complain about his back hurting. Since he had had back surgery in the late 1980s, he thought he had strained his back. After a few weeks, he went to the doctor and was told that it was nothing serious and was given some pain medication. The pain persisted and then he experienced what could only be called constipation. Since this had been the case after his back surgery, he was not too concerned. Finally, when the pain intensified, on August 17th he drove himself to the emergency room. Usually a medical diagnosis takes numerous tests extended over a period of time, but one MRI on that day determined that Bob had seven tumors in his pancreas and liver. The doctor minced no words about the prognosis—Bob had pancreatic cancer with six months to live.

I always considered Bob a pessimist because he often spoke of dying young. Throughout our marriage he fought heart disease and endured a quintuple bypass at the age of 48. We all assumed that a heart attack would be the cause of his death. When he was diagnosed with pancreatic cancer at age 56, it took all of us by surprise.

Pancreatic cancer is one of the deadliest forms of cancer because normally when you get symptoms, it is too late. This was the case with Bob. When you get news like this you can't wrap your brain around it. Every fiber of your being goes into denial. As long as there is life, there is hope and you cling to any hope, however slight. His doctor told us about an experimental chemotherapy study and he signed up. We both refused to give in to this cancer.

During his illness, I went to work sporadically. I would go when he felt good and stay home with him when he didn't. I went to every chemo session with him. Going through chemotherapy is a scary and horrible experience and I wanted to be with him each time. You sit there for hours while a poison flows through you, hoping it will kill the cancer. Sometimes the intended cure seems worse than the disease. There were many days when the source of his discomfort was not the cancer but the chemo.

Most of the time you simply try to function because that is all you can do. We spent many hours driving around looking at houses being built in our area and just being together. I thought that we still had time together because we never ever sat down and talked about his death. The reality of his impending death never really sank in with him or me. I thought it just wouldn't happen. When the hospice nurse asked if he had any funeral arrangements, Bob said "No, I sure don't. We are both in denial, thank you very much."

Bob, even while sick, was still busy with his little projects. Over the years, our normal routine was that I was the go-fer and he was the fixer. He kept me running around town doing his errands. I think he was so afraid that his life was over that this was his way of maintaining hope. There were many times I did not feel like I could continue the pace. I just wanted to sit down and be with him, yet to do so would seem to him like I was losing hope. To this day, I regret that time together slipped away. There are so many things that I wanted to say to him.

Our day-to-day existence was focused on Bob and his condition, the kids, and how they were dealing with his illness and generally just trying to maintain some normalcy. We had friends and family constantly calling for information and I was in and out of school, depending on how Bob felt. Each day was full of hope, yet each night I would get in the shower and cry my eyes out when Bob could not see or hear me. The tragic events of September 11 changed the world, yet it had little impact on us. I remember it happening but felt absolutely nothing. The brain is an amazing organ. It knew that I had no room for anything else. All my thoughts and emotions were so focused on what was going on in our life.

As if my life was not stressful enough, I was also dealing with my mother. In 2000, she had been diagnosed with Alzheimer's. My sister, Joy Patterson, and I decided to move her to our area so that we could take care of her. It had come to the point where she could no longer live alone and it took both of us to tend to her needs. After Bob's diagnosis, my wonderful sister immediately insisted that she would assume all of Mama's care. Even though that was a tremendous relief, the concern for my mother was ever present.

For most of this time, Bob's physical condition was dependent on his chemotherapy. His major problem was the discomfort from the chemo. After about seven weeks of treatment, he started to go downhill. At first it was just minor pain, but then he started to become disoriented and unresponsive. The doctor told us he was experiencing liver failure. Another MRI showed that he now had 26 tumors.

Bob died on October 12, 2001, exactly eight weeks to the day after he was diagnosed. Fortunately, pancreatic cancer is quick and merciful. There was little pain until the last few days. He died at home with his family around him. Mecca had moved home to help me take care of him. Hayden was also there when she could be. At Bob's insistence, Rachel had left for college a week after his diagnosis. When Bob's condition deteriorated, we called Rachel and she drove the four hours home. I believe Bob waited until everyone was there before he died.

The next two weeks I was in a daze. You go through the funeral arrangements, visitation and funeral like you are in a fog. You say all the things that you know people expect to hear and do all the things you're expected to do. Reality doesn't sink in. You keep expecting things to go back to the way they were, but they don't.

About a week and a half after Bob died, I had to let it all out. I told my children that I needed to be alone. I needed time to be by myself. That is when I let my grief out. I know that everyone handles grief differently, but in my case I had to just let the emotions flow—however it happened. I cried non-stop for three days. The release of all the emotion of the past two and a half months came tumbling out. No one had ever told me that grief could manifest itself through physical pain, but my body literally hurt. I could never have imagined that much intensity of grief.

Becoming a widow at any age is difficult, but at 49 it was so unexpected. I went back to work two weeks after Bob died. In reality, that is not enough time, but I had no choice. Being busy during the day, however, ended up being good for me as it kept my mind occupied and made the time pass. For the first few months I think I was still in some form of shock. That time period is still a fog in my memory.

For months I was busy with the "business of death." No one prepares you for the onslaught of paperwork that one faces. You have to do all the necessary things that accompany the death of a spouse. This involves all kinds of financial arrangements, from sending out death certificates to numerous places, refinancing the house, changing your tax status, medical bills and changing all manner of business arrangements into your name. In a way it was good therapy to take my mind off things. But yet, the business of life still looms over you. All I can say is that "you do what you have to do." That phrase best describes my coping mechanism.

I'll never forget a phone conversation I had when I tried to cancel a cell phone contract that was in Bob's name. They kept insisting that they could not terminate the contract until they spoke to Bob. When I explained that he had passed away, they still insisted that they could do nothing until they spoke to him. At one point I became so exasperated that I finally told them, "Look, if you get in touch with him, let me know because there are some things that I need to ask him."

How does one go about coping with such a total life changing event? I went from a busy wife and mother to an empty house and nothing. Overnight my life had changed drastically.

The previous year had been one of the busiest ones of my life. At the time, Rachel was a senior in high school and an officer on her drill team. With everything from a trip to New York City for her to march in the Macy's Thanksgiving Day Parade, competing in national dance competitions, and all kinds of fund-raising activities, the entire year was a whirlwind.

Then within a couple of months, I went from all that to absolutely nothing. My husband was gone. Rachel was 200 miles away in college, Mecca and Hayden had their own lives, and my home— once full of kids and life—was now empty. That also describes how I felt inside.

For months after Bob died I had difficulty sleeping. Sometimes I wanted to let my broken heart take over. I was full of all kinds of questions about my future, as well as doubts about whether or not I could make it by myself. There were moments when I simply did not want to get up in the morning and face the day—but I did. I guess I could have chosen to wallow in self pity and grief but that is not who I am. You simply "do what you have to do." If you can't handle death, you can't handle life. I have always considered myself to be a strong person but I never really knew how strong I was until Bob died. I have never been one to lie down and feel sorry for myself and this situation was no different.

I have always had a strong faith and that faith, along with my family and friends, is what sustained me during this difficult time. If I had believed in no heaven or afterlife, I truly believe that the grief would have overcome me. I wonder how those people who don't share that belief can cope with the finality of death. My faith has always taught me that there is a heaven and through Jesus we will all see our departed loved ones again. I can only imagine how horrible it must feel to think that you will never see your loved ones again. On many occasions, I have felt Bob's presence with me. I feel like he is up there watching over me. My belief in God and knowing that Bob is up there with him still sustains me. I know I will see him again.

I have a wonderful family and friends who are there for me with their love and presence. I get up each morning for them and for me. The saying "life goes on" sounds trite but is really quite true. You can't just lie down and die yourself. To do so would be quite selfish and hurt the ones you love. Life does go on and you have to choose to live it.

I must have done something right because I have always heard that part of one's measure of a good life is the friends one has. Good friends are rare. I have been especially blessed in that I have had not one, but two, best friends since I was ten years old. Karan Armstrong and Frances Hamm have nurtured a friendship that has evolved into more of a "sisterhood" over the years. They have always been my rock and coping with Bob's death was no different. They were both there for me throughout his illness and death, and their love and support helped me get through it. I will forever be indebted to them and treasure their friendship more each day.

I have grown up with dogs and cats. They are not mere pets, but more like members of the family. Throughout our marriage, Bob and I always had numerous pets. We raised our children to love animals and all our pets were very much a part of our lives. My dogs were true friends to me in my time of grief. I don't believe that I could have made it without their undying affection and unconditional love. Their company gave me comfort many long and lonely nights and they are still a very large part of my life. I can't imagine life without them.

It has been almost five years since Bob died. I miss him. I will always miss him. I think about him every day. There are still those times when I want to tell him something so badly I can hardly stand it. I want to know what he thinks about something or share some idea that I have. That will never change. I will never get over it. One simply gets through it.

Like every mother in this situation, I have regrets for our children. Bob's death affected them in ways that only the future will tell. He will never see our youngest daughter Rachel graduate from college. He was not there to walk his beautiful daughter Mecca down the aisle or meet his new son-in-law, Cory. In January of 2006, Mecca gave birth to a wonderful little boy named Merrick. He will never know his grandfather except for the stories that we tell him. Rachel and Hayden will not have their father present for such important life events. I know there is no way I can compensate them for this loss.

I know my children worry about me being alone. Yes, I live alone, but I am not lonely. I have my dogs, large and small, to keep me company and provide protection. I have friends and neighbors who are always there for me. I get lonesome on occasion, but doesn't everyone? Quite frankly, I enjoy my solitude.

If I had to offer any advice on how to deal with such a massive change, it would have to be to choose to live life to its fullest and not look back. Part of life is dealing with the death of loved ones. I lost both my grandmothers in my early twenties. My father died in 1987 at the age of 74 and in December of 2003, I lost my mother, who was 87. The loss of a parent is difficult yet not the same as losing a spouse. I had the wonderful example that my mother set after my father died. She never looked back and embraced life with all her normal exuberance. She taught me that faith and family are the most important things in life.

I now understand much of what my grandmother and mother said about remarriage as a widow. Neither of them showed any interest in remarrying. Even though my grandmother also became a widow at the young age of 45, she said that she would never remarry. At this point in my life, I can honestly say that I feel the same way. I may change my mind later, but right now, and for the last five years, another marriage is the last thing on my mind. Many other widows with whom I have talked have shared the same sentiment. For myself, I enjoy my independence and autonomy.

Sometimes I worry about the future. When Bob was alive, we had a plan, or at least thought we did. We were going to retire from teaching and live our golden years with wonderful activities. We were looking forward to spoiling our grandchildren, traveling and enjoying all those things retired people do. Now that Bob is gone, sometimes I feel uncertain about my future. I have been teaching for 32 years and plan to retire in two or three years. After retirement, I am not sure about many things. I know that I want to be close to my children and their families, but I do not want to live my life through them or be a burden to them. I need to be my own person. Exactly what that involves is still a question.

Bob's death was traumatic and painful. But, I have learned that how we deal with adversity is our choice. I have been blessed with a husband I loved, children that bring me joy, and a faith that makes it possible to face my future with the knowledge that I am not alone. I have a full life with family, friends, my animals, and a lifelong career that has brought me fulfillment. Who could ask for more in their bonus years?

It has been a revelation that I have the power to make myself happy.

A Closing Thought From Ben and Ken

There are few things more debilitating than grief. When an individual is in its grasp, grief can become the core of a person's existence and make life a day-to-day struggle.

Gay has discovered that it is still within her power to live through her grief and continue with life. She's surrounded herself with faith, family, friends, and career as a way to stand against the darkness. From those gifts she's found strength and compassion for her own wellness.

Grief is an inevitable part of life. If you haven't lost someone you love, it's just because you haven't lived long enough. Grief is an intensely personal thing. For some, the pain is visible and vocal... for others, the hurt is internalized and silent. The crucial thing is for you to find someone you trust with whom to share your feelings ... a friend, pastor, rabbi, counselor, or your physician. It is an unfortunate fact our bonus years will have grief associated with them. We still can find the joy of living every day to the highest potential as a buffer for the times of grief we face.

The scripture brings us hope, too. "Cast all your anxiety on him because he cares for you" (1 Peter 5:7).

Chapter 10

CHASE AND EMBRACE YOUR CHAZOWN!
Lance Robertson

An Introduction

All of us former athletes instantly connect with the title and theme of this book. In this context, it is such an appropriate analogy for our lives, particularly our careers. The spirit of overtime—a fresh opportunity, a second chance—is exhilarating. The heart beats faster, energy levels are renewed and each moment becomes precious. Additionally, I like thinking about overtime as meaning that nothing previously accomplished matters in terms of your success. You could have scored five touchdowns and ran for 250 yards. Doesn't matter. One fumble and it could be over. Interestingly enough, you start all over again, per se, but with an unmatched intensity. You play (or approach your career) now like never before. Where would we be if we started our careers with that intensity?

My story is probably not unique but I feel my response has been, after talking with many colleagues and friends. I hope after reading this chapter you will find some positive, encouraging tidbits you can use as you venture forth.

The Background

Dr. Ben Dickerson, a longtime friend and mentor, in his initial letter asking us to contribute a chapter to this book, wrote, "In today's society, people will do about anything to maintain their security and status. They'll stay in unhappy marriages, keep a job they hate, and avoid making changes of any kind." Reflecting on that statement, I realized that had been me! Let me clarify— personally I was (am) a very blessed man. I have a beautiful, supportive wife and two incredible little girls. God has been very good, providing far more than I deserve.

Professionally, however, I had been unhappy and visionless. I had dedicated 12 years of my career to higher education, working at a major university in Oklahoma. I started off working in outreach (continuing education) in 1994 and a few years later I was appointed to director of that outreach unit for the college I was in. I thoroughly enjoyed the work and made significant contributions to the unit's ongoing success. During my tenure as director, the unit experienced unparalleled growth. The unit offered hundreds of programs annually, serving many thousands of Oklahomans. Our unit played a critical, multifunctional role within the college. Beyond outreach efforts, we managed development activities, marketing, distance education, publications and supplemental credit course offerings. Also, we generated millions in grant dollars. We won countless awards for our successes. We were proud, rightfully so, for the impact we were having on the community and the pillar of strength we were to the college.

During that time, I began to hone in on what would become my area of great interest and specialization: gerontology. Given the strong role my grandparents played in my upbringing, I had a natural inclination toward helping older adults. Even prior to becoming director of outreach I had worked concurrently with a colleague to create the university's gerontology institute. We developed great programs that served family caregivers, grandparents raising grandchildren, and professionals in the field of aging.

I gave everything to my job, my university, my alma mater. It actually became more than a job. I allowed it, as I learned to regret later, to consume me. I correlated my value as a professional to what I accomplished in that job.

The Change

Then, that historic day came—a day that radically altered my outlook on work. The saga occurs often in higher education. A new president arrives and feels the instantaneous need to start making changes, cutting programs, reallocating funding, and turning everything upside down. That's what happened at my institution and one of the items on the chopping block was outreach. No matter how many reports generated in argument of our continued existence, each incredibly compelling, that inevitable day came.

In September 2005, I was called into my dean's office and told that outreach was no longer a priority and we were not a good fit in their new puzzle. Twelve distinguished years of service, countless successes, and undying loyalty all meant nothing. It was an incredible punch in the stomach. I was shocked. My family and friends were shocked.

So, my change, although forced upon me, was to leave higher education and embark on a journey of self discovery. The question I kept asking myself: Where do I go from here?

The Consequences of My Change

You see, this was all part of God's plan. (That is always easier said looking back than forward.) They say most life changing moments are realized as such later. But, I know now that I should have left that position years ago. God had been training me, making me knowledgeable, and preparing me to find and embrace my "chazown." I was complacent and stagnant. I had no vision. And, it was time for a change.

Let me interject here and explain chazown. Proverbs 29:18 (KJV) says, "Where there is no vision, the people perish: but he that keepth the law, happy is he."

My church pastor, Craig Groeschel, once lectured on the Hebrew word for vision—chazown (khaw-zone). Although he was using it in a biblical context, does it not apply to us both professionally and personally? With no vision, we "perish."

Leaving the world you know and making a major career change can be scary, difficult and complex. However, there comes a time when you no longer fear the risk. You'd rather flip hamburgers than continue down a meaningless path. That's when you ask yourself: What makes me come alive? What stirs my heart?

My perspective now, since my change, is completely different than before. I am approaching things with a new sense of determination, cherishing each moment and trying to make each step with the big picture in mind.

I would be foolish to say that everything associated with the change was pleasant. Being completely honest, the challenges can be daunting. My immediate response was somewhat polarized. Some moments I felt worthless and felt like I had failed. I felt stupid for not being more prepared and for being somewhat naïve. I felt taken advantage of and was filled with bitterness. Initially, it can shatter you.

Other moments were euphoric, knowing I was free to reinvent myself. I can relate it to the definition of overtime I mentioned at the beginning of the chapter. You get to start this new phase of your life with unmatched intensity, erasing events of the past. I felt excited, ambitious, confident and ready.

Fortunately, I quickly embraced the second set of emotions. Through prayer, encouragement by family and friends, and a strong resolve, I am back on track—even stronger than before. God had paved the way financially, however, with the growing success of my wife's company. During my trials and tribulations, I could tell she wasn't sure what to do or say. But, she did the very thing I needed by listening and loving.

My Current Status

Since my change last fall, I have been blessed to be able to identify and chase my *chazown*. Elaborated more below, this experience has given me such clarity about what I want with my future. Chiefly, I have absolutely no desire to ever work for anyone else again. I am proudly self employed, building my own consulting business and working on several of my passions. I work from home, spend loads of time with my family, and enjoy every minute of every day. Also, I am involved in helping my wife with her network marketing company, which God has greatly blessed.

Last but not least, I have been able to dedicate time to a longtime passion of mine. As a gerontologist, I have wanted to create a meaningful program that would help family caregivers. We have nearly 44 million family caregivers in our country—individuals who often balance responsibilities at work and as parents and spouses while caring for a loved one. At this point, there are few programs in place to help these individuals find much needed respite (relief, a break from care giving duties). With the help of colleagues, we have launched a national foundation called the National Omega Care Foundation, which will provide vouchers to family caregivers redeemable for in-home, non-medical, holistic care, giving them the help they desperately need but often can't afford.

What I Learned

Reflecting on the last nine months, I could write an entire book on what I learned. Some lessons were new for me, others reiterations of what I already knew. Thankfully, I can honestly say that these lessons are now deeply embedded in who I am and who I hope to become someday. This recent period of time has afforded me the opportunity to reinvent myself, very critically, which can be both pleasurable and painful.

I hope what I share in this chapter and what you're reading throughout the book encourage you to learn, grow and take risks. Change can be difficult, but it can result in unparalleled wisdom. For brevity's sake, I've clustered what I have learned through my experience into four major themes. These lessons, or guiding points, apply to us all, regardless of where you are at in your profession or the severity of the change you are considering. They have shaped me. Apply them and they will shape you.

1. Have a Game Plan

First and foremost, I learned how important it is to have a game plan. With no game plan, we just stumble along blindly, naïve to how dispensable we have become. Let's revisit the verse in Proverbs: "Where there is no vision....the people perish." Do you have a vision? If you do, and the fact that you are taking the time to read this book probably indicates you just might, then start building a game plan to accomplish your vision. Write it down. Sketch it out. This is absolutely essential. Everything will start falling into place once you do. You've likely heard the startling statistic that only seven percent of Americans have goals. Remember this: Those who do not have goals often work for those who do. Which end of that equation do you want to be on?

My wife and I are in the process now of building our life plan. That's right—a plan that outlines everything we want to achieve, how we will get there, and how long it will take. Of course, we will adjust it as time goes along to better capture our shifting desires. But, it is a great start! The process alone has been inspiring and I encourage you (and spouse, if applicable) to do it. Remember, desire reveals design and design reveals destiny.

Someone once said, "This one step, choosing a goal and sticking to it, changes everything." I now believe that. So many people feel stuck, unable to move, or paralyzed. If you want to change your situation, develop a plan and take action.

2. Aim Higher

Why is it our nature to settle for less than we deserve? Why are we so easily emasculated? Why do we fear taking risks? A life lived in fear is no life at all. You know you want more. God wants to give you more. As a matter of fact, according to Mylon LeFevre's book, *How Blessed Do You Want to Be? Make the Choice That Makes the Difference*, "God wants you to prosper in all facets of your life. When you prosper from trusting in the Lord, it shows the world what a good God you serve. He gets the glory for the good things in your life when you openly trust him, and others are drawn to him because they see how good he is to you."

LeFevre also notes that prosperity is a condition of the heart. Although my efforts are still in their infancy stages, I am thrilled to tell you that I am healthy, free from fear, and blessed to be a blessing! Now that is real prosperity! I want to give the world more than I am taking out. I want people to prosper spiritually, physically, emotionally, mentally, relationally, and financially. God wants to bless you so you can be a blessing.

As you build your vision and plan, aim high. We were created to explore, build and conquer. The book *Wild at Heart* by John Eldredge is one of my all-time favorite books. He says, "A man must have a battle to fight, a great mission to his life that involves and yet transcends even home and family. He must have a cause to which he is devoted even unto death, for this is written into the fabric of his being." Doesn't that send a chill down your spine? Yes, it is incredibly bold and maybe a little sensational, but it sure challenges me to elevate my level of thinking a notch or two! How about you?

Likewise, Eldredge encourages his readers to "start choosing to live out your strength and you'll discover that it grows each time. Begin to taste your true strength and you'll want more."

So, if you had permission to do what you really want to do, what would you do? Don't ask *how*; that will cut your desire off at the knees. How is a faithless question. How is God's department. He is asking you *what*.

- What is written in your heart?
- What makes you come alive?
- What have you always wanted to do?

Leo Burnett, a famous businessman and legendary advertising icon, once said, "When you reach for the stars you may not quite get one, but you won't come up with a handful of mud either." Aim high.

3. Trust Yourself

Another great lesson I learned was to be loyal to yourself and to trust your instincts and abilities. Sadly, most people don't believe in themselves. We have been conditioned to adopt our employer's opinion of us, to not make mistakes, to not take risks. You are more valuable than your employer says and God made you to take risks. My daughters were taught in school, "If you can't make mistakes, you can't make anything."

Know who you are and know your strengths. Know, understand, take pride in, practice, develop, use, exploit and enjoy your greatest strengths. The world offers a man a false sense of power and a false sense of security.

4. Prepare for Turbulence, Failure and Success

There is such a fine line between success and failure. Often, your attitude makes the difference. When Thomas Edison was asked, after so many failures to successfully invent the light bulb, how he felt about all the time and energy he wasted on ideas that didn't work, he simply said, *"The way I look at it is now I know of a thousand ways not to invent a light bulb."*

For some of you, like me, change is forced upon you. Roll with it! Learn, grow, renew your resolve, and plunge ahead. British writer Aldous Huxley once said, "You cannot control what happens to you, but you can control your attitude towards what happens to you, and in that, you will be mastering change rather than allowing it to master you."

It has been said that God rigged the world in such a way that it only works when we embrace risk as the theme of our lives, which is to say only when we live by faith. We know the Bible tells us God will never leave us nor forsake us. My favorite verse, which I recite often in turbulent, uncertain times, is Jeremiah 29:11: "For I know the plans I have for you," declares the Lord, "plans to prosper you and not to harm you, plans to give you hope and a future."

There comes a time when we simply have to face the challenges in our lives and stop backing down. It can be scary. Fear and honor go hand in hand. There will be times when things don't go well. During the turbulence, remember these key tidbits:

- First, I will say in hindsight some advice a mentor of mine gave me was important. Always keep your cool. When difficult situations arise, as they did in my case, don't lose control. When you lose control—well, you don't actually lose it, you give it away—you can count on an undesirable outcome.
- Be strong and endure. As you work through problems one step at a time, you will strengthen your habits of endurance and

increase your confidence for the next challenge. Use each day's opportunities to build endurance and accomplish the immediate objective. The great Walt Disney said, "Success has nothing to do with intelligence and everything to do with pursuit."

- Likewise, persist and be patient. We are all faced with a series of great opportunities brilliantly disguised as insoluble problems. Things that last usually require more time and determination than usual. When God wants to make an oak tree, he takes 60 years. When he wants to make a mushroom, he takes six hours. Do you want to be an oak tree or a mushroom? Herbert Kaufman once said, "The habit of persistence is the habit of victory."

My definitions of success and failure have now changed as well. To me, it's not about how much money you make, promotions, or possessions. It's about the ultimate freedom. Freedom from others controlling you. Freedom to pick your path and determine your destiny. Freedom to do something that makes a difference.

Just remember, as my favorite football coach the former Chicago Bears coach Mike Ditka, once said, "Success is never permanent, and failure is never final."

Now, let me quickly discuss another lesson I learned and took to heart, although I didn't include it in the listing because this may not be for everyone. The greatest lesson I learned—which I like to think of as a personal epiphany—is that I will likely not experience true freedom working for someone else. The above lessons naturally led into this acknowledgement. I feel strongly that for me to be truly successful and free I must work for myself, rely on my own abilities, build a residual income base and closely follow a strategic path to success.

In today's business world, it's an unfortunate fact that many employers will only pay their workers the minimum required to keep them on the job. The reciprocal of that business model is that many employees will only work hard enough to keep from being fired. Often there doesn't seem to be any corporate or employee loyalty. Where's the victory in that equation? If we are truly living in a state of "overtime," then we should be very selective about who calls the plays, right? Have we not been learning, mastering certain skills, and building a solid track record? We know ourselves better than anyone—both our strengths and weaknesses. Again, this is just my opinion. My experience has really caused me to think deeply about putting my talents on the line for an employer and the vulnerability sometimes associated with that decision.

Now, this sort of aspiration can be scary stuff. It takes courage. S. J. Rachman, a Canadian psychologist specializing in fear and courage, says that many people think of courage as fearlessness. However, Rachman defines courage similarly as "perseverance in the face of fear and stress." Courage is a personal strength, which equates to the ability to act. Wow! That is powerful! Can you imagine tackling life with that sort of attitude?

Questions I Pose To You

After reading this book and this chapter, I hope you've already begun forming and somewhat addressing the questions that naturally arise as you assimilate the information shared by the various authors. The questions I pose to you:

- What makes you come alive?
  "Don't ask yourself what the world needs. Ask yourself what makes you come alive, and go do that, because what the world needs is people who have come alive." —Gil Bailie, Christian author
- Do you have a vision?
  "Everybody ends up somewhere, but few end up somewhere on purpose." —Craig Groeschel, senior pastor, LifeChurch.tv
- What's holding you back from changing?
  "Confidence comes not from always being right but from not fearing to be wrong." —Author unknown
- What's the worst that could happen if you make this change?
  "The only thing that stands between a man and what he wants from life is often merely the will to try it and the faith to believe that it is possible." —Author unknown
- What will happen if you don't?

"One of life's failures is people who did not realize how close they were to success when they gave up." —Thomas Edison

Books I Would Recommend You Read

I am a huge believer in self development. Invest in yourself and it will pay big dividends. First and foremost, reading God's word will build your faith and keep you free from doubts and fears that would otherwise destroy your success. Beyond biblical devotions, some great books I would happily recommend to you, in no particular order, include:

- *Wild at Heart* — John Eldredge. One of the best books I have ever read. Although it is designed to challenge growth in a man, its application is universal. John challenges us to be warriors and embrace adventure.
- *Today Matters* — John Maxwell. An excellent book that highlights John's recommended 12 daily practices to guarantee tomorrow's success.
- *How Blessed Do You Want to Be? Make the Choice That Makes the Difference* — Mylon LeFevre. This award winning Christian musician wrote this simple book that reminds us that God has far more blessings than we have needs.
- *Chazown* — Craig Groeschel. A newly released book that is sure to inspire, focusing on the importance of having a vision.
- *The Blessings of Favor* — Kate McVeigh. This encouraging book reminds us that the more we acknowledge God's favor in our lives, the more we will see it.

Conclusion

If you are unhappy and dissatisfied with your lot in life, make the change. Yes, it can be scary. But, your breakthrough is around the corner.

I believe, for the brief time we are here on earth, we were created to do something meaningful. That may require leaving your comfort zone and making a change. It will certainly require you to identify your chazown. That vision should provide clarity and, hopefully, a path. I leave you with an inspiring quote from former President Woodrow Wilson: "You are not here merely to make a living. You are here in order to enable the world to live more amply, with greater vision, with a finer spirit of hope and achievement. You are here to enrich the world, and you impoverish yourself if you forget that errand." Here's to chasing and embracing your chazown!

A Closing Thought From Ben and Ken

Lance knows what every great track star understands: Looking back slows you down and can make you stumble. It doesn't help you reach the goal and can even hinder you. Leaving behind the disappointment Lance faced in his university role, he started a new path for his bonus years. He refused to look back at those who did not share his vision and instead looked forward to a new career that would give him the freedom of work he always sought.

Likewise, you may well have encountered situations that stifled you and crushed your ambitions. Don't allow the anger and hurt of those situations to hold you back. Take a hint from the runner who is sprinting to reach the finish line, don't look back ... keep your eye on the goal. You'll find perseverance is a great virtue. Don't give up, don't look back, the future is in front of you and it's a great one.

DO YOU KNOW WHERE YOU ARE NOW?
Lou Stoops

Do you know where you are now? It's a simple question my mother used to ask me every time we rode the city buses in our town. I guess she just wanted me to pay attention to my surroundings so that I would be better able to navigate my way around. She would point out certain landmarks along the route and then tell me something that made that place special. On the next trip along that route when we neared the landmark she would ask, "Do you know where you are now?" By the age of 12, I could easily travel our town without being confused or getting lost.

Navigating city streets is one thing; navigating life is another. At the age of 40, I went through a pretty troubling time. I began to become restless about my life. I felt uneasy about my professional accomplishments; I had many dreams and aspirations that I was nowhere near realizing. I wasn't unhappy. I had a wonderful wife (still do) and three wonderful children and I was working at a vocation that I truly felt called toward (still do) earning a good but modest income. I just felt that something was missing and I had to do something about it.

I had been working for 20 years as a pastor. I enjoyed my work but where I was professionally didn't fully match up to who I was at that time in life. Some might chalk it up to a mid-life crisis. Well, maybe. I did realize that I wasn't getting any younger and if I was to do something about my career then I would have to get started.

I wasn't looking to change careers. My story is about seeking career expansion. I wanted to venture into new directions while continuing the work I was already engaged in. I felt there was no need to follow conventional "wisdom" that sticks a person in a box and says, "This is who you are and what you can do." I felt, and still feel, that we can be many things at once and there is no need to be fastened down to only one career path. Though I still feel that way and am still busy pursuing the many and diverse career interests that engage my imagination, I now understand that doing so isn't easy.

I had worked all my professional life as a pastor. By the time I was 40, I was serving my fourth church. I love the work even though there is no end to the politics of a local church, I still see myself as a pastor. Even so, I wanted to branch out. I wanted to work in the full arena of media. I love to be creative through writing, acting and speaking. I wanted to work in television and radio; to speak for corporations; to write for newspapers, magazines and author books. I knew that I could do more and I passionately wanted to try.

My hope was to begin efforts to broaden my career so that in a short period of time I would have replaced my salary as a pastor. I could then continue serving as a pastor, no longer being tied to a church for my income. I value financial freedom independent of the church, so I set out to work toward that end. I had always said, "Someday I'm going to…" Now "someday" was upon me.

I began by reading everything I could get my hands on written by individuals who were doing what I wanted to do. I read books and articles, taking a sort of crash course, absorbing as much knowledge as possible so that I could launch out on my own. I not only read all I could, I also contacted people in my community who were successful at those careers I was interested in. I figured that by asking them two questions I might save time and trouble along the way. I asked them, "What did you do that worked and why?" and "What did you do that didn't work and why?" I reasoned that those two questions were "cut to the chase" in nature, teaching me just about everything I would need to know to have a smooth trip in the expansion of my own career.

After I had done all this over a span of six months, I began to take the steps necessary to get where I wanted to go. Knowledge is power and with knowledge I launched out. I had read that to be a successful professional speaker or author you must first become famous. Corporations like to hire speakers that people have already heard of and publishers like to publish writers that are well known, already having a built-in market. So, to do either I had to become famous. It's kind of like needing a loan from a bank; you must first prove you don't need one in order to get one.

I started by coming up with an idea for a column that would be suitable for newspapers, magazines and the web. It had to be short and sweet. No more than four or five hundred words max. It had to pack a punch and provide real value to the reader. I came up with the concept of a column focusing on positive answers to personal and professional issues people faced daily. I would use historical references to illustrate each column as well as my own personal experiences. The tone would be upbeat and the target market would be business people and entrepreneurs. I titled the column *Positively Speaking*.

I compiled about ten sample columns and began the process of sending them out to publications that fit the targeted market. It proved to be difficult but I finally heard from a newspaper that wanted to run the column weekly. They had liked it and thought it was a perfect fit for their employment publication.

I was now off and running. As time passed the column was picked up by a number of websites and a national magazine. In a little over a year of effort I had managed to gain a readership base of one million people! The national exposure began to open doors for me. I started getting speaking requests from various groups, mostly local service clubs at first. Community service clubs are populated with business people and business owners that have the power to hire speakers. The service clubs were free but the referrals paid a fee!

In a little over a year and a half I became known as an able motivational and informational speaker, as well as a popular columnist. My journey to expand my career was off and rolling. I was traveling far and fast, but I still felt it wasn't far and fast enough. I needed to increase my efforts by becoming a published author. You see, books are crucial for professional speakers since two-thirds of a speaker's income results from back-of-the room sales. I had to create something that would be an income stream and a book made sense.

Earlier during a speaking event I attended, I had met a man who worked as an acquisition editor for a major publishing house. I contacted him to pitch my ideas for a potential book. We met for coffee, and after talking awhile he indicated that he was interested in publishing my columns in a compilation book. Who was I to argue with genius? "Great," I said, and off we went. In a matter of a few short months from our coffee encounter, I was a published author! Now, I thought, opportunities and money would come flying in.

I soon discovered that becoming a published author was one thing—becoming a *successful* published author was another. In order to create a "buzz" for a new book, the author has to be "out there" making personal appearances, getting interviews and being a key player in the marketing process. Okay, I thought, I'm game. I had no problem in promoting my work. After all, if it's worth doing it's worth promoting.

I began to call anybody and everybody I knew in media and, in the process, spoke with a segment producer for a new local morning news show debuting on the Fox Television Network affiliate in my city. I told her that I had a new book to promote and I also worked as a columnist and speaker. She gladly asked me to make an appearance and I gladly said "YES."

I knew one appearance would not lead to a sales bonanza for my book but I was excited. I did the interview and it went well—but what next? I had to keep going to create the buzz. As I fumbled my way through my rolodex attempting to score another interview, the phone rang. The segment producer was calling me to ask if I would like to come on again and speak about a workplace problem for their audience. "Yes, I would be happy to," I responded. After an additional two appearances, she asked me to become a regular feature on the show, appearing weekly as the "Monday Motivator." The one-shot appearance turned into a four year run on a popular morning show and I just knew I was on my way; this career-expansion thing was taking off!

It was during this time I secured an agent to represent me for commercial television work. I started doing one commercial and then another, and soon I was doing industrial videos and voice-over spots as well. Everything I wanted to do I was doing. I was moving along at break-neck speed on my career-expansion trip and I was sure I would soon arrive at my destination: financial independence. I would be able to serve as a pastor with no need for money as a concern, while doing everything else I enjoyed.

With all my opportunities in play, I decided to leave my full-time job as a pastor. I had been ten years at the church and I had felt my work there was done. I wasn't intending on leaving my pastoral career forever; I did intend to "retire" from serving as a paid employee. Truthfully, I was tired of all the politics that come with professional ministry and I would be in a better position to make a lasting impact if I could separate my livelihood from it. I also wanted to build upon my success in media, seeing how far I could go.

It looked like blue skies and smooth traveling lay ahead; after all, I was speaking regularly, becoming more and better known. Surely it would continue unabated, I thought. My wife and I were in agreement about leaving my job and launching out toward new vistas of opportunity. We both felt it was time. So we set a date of departure, and off we went.

I started accelerating my efforts to go farther and faster while taking an interim position with a church that was itself in transition. The interim church would give additional freedom and require a fraction of my time. It was a good move, but it only lasted seven months. No problem, I thought. I still felt pretty secure in my career expansion efforts and was confident it would continue to be smooth traveling ahead. Little did I know that things were about to drastically change, and not for the better.

It didn't take long after I left the interim work to realize I might have made a big mistake. Perhaps I had been a tad bit hasty in leaving my full-time position a little over seven months earlier. It soon became obvious to me that I needed an anchor income. A month or so after leaving the interim position I knew I was in trouble.

My speaking engagements began to taper off and my book sales weren't booming; except for my commercial work, the television career wasn't providing any real income either. People around me thought I was doing really well; after all, I was an author, speaker and on television every week. I most certainly must be rolling in the loot! My wife is fond of saying, "I wish we were as rich as everybody thinks we are." The truth was far from the perception! We were stopped alongside the road to our dreams. My career expansion was imploding.

In the ensuing months I found myself lost as to what to do next. I had come too far to get stuck now. I hadn't a clue how to jumpstart things and get back on track. My creative juices dried up as mounting economic troubles began to put the squeeze on me. I began to become depressed, feeling the dryness of burnout as I saw no way clear in forward movement. I tried everything I knew, but nothing worked. This went on for two years until I finally decided once again to take a full-time ministry position.

My wife and I had survived, but just barely. Returning to the full-time pastoral ministry felt like a defeat even though I knew the work to be noble. I set out in this new work to make a difference, approaching it with determination. I would continue my multiple career paths but I would slow down and smell the roses a bit more.

I considered myself a lot more realistic than I had been before; it became clear that I would need to be more realistic. After two years of working in my new position I found myself again unemployed. Politics are prevalent and a constant force in church life; if any man dares to do such work he had better resign himself to that fact. I did.

I was now in search of stability once more. To pursue my career expansion I had to find another income anchor. A friend of mine had just purchased a recreational vehicle dealership and asked if I would come and work for him. Considering my alternatives I said, "Yes!"

I was especially motivated to accept because the station I had been doing the weekly segments for decided that they wanted to "go in a different direction." That can be translated as "goodbye." Also, the newspaper and national magazine I was writing for went out of business. Without the exposure from these sources my speaking career was almost completely stalled. I was out of gas on the road to my dreams. My mother's question, *Do you know where you are now?* could only be answered by, "Yes, I'm at an RV dealership!"

My friend who had hired me had hoped I would be a great service manager. Well, he soon saw that that wasn't going to be proven true. He gave me a position in marketing, which was more in line with my experience. Even so, after a year of doing marketing the dealership went under. I found myself, again, numbered among the unemployed. I was more upbeat this time. Surely things will soon get better. I still see myself as an optimist, albeit a learned one.

It was seven months from leaving the dealership when things began to change for the better. I was asked to speak at a church where I had spoken some years earlier. It was a multiethnic church that had been without a full-time pastor for seven years. I filled in for several months and then began to think that this was truly a work I would enjoy. The challenges would be immense but I felt ready to once again serve. I had no clue as to their ability to pay a salary but I wanted to give it a go. I took the position as pastor and it has proven to be an oasis in the midst of what had been a very dry desert.

Now it would be understandable to think that I might have good cause to abandon any thought toward career expansion after having failed so miserably. Well, the simple truth is that I'm more enthused and determined than ever. Even though I've experienced great disappointment and failure, I've also achieved great success. I subscribed to what Dolly Parton once said when asked by someone as to how she had managed to keep going after setbacks and disappointments. She said, "I've never stopped trying and I've never tried stopping!"

Along this journey of mine I've managed to observe some key landmarks and notice the signs that I believe result in a greater wisdom than I had when I began. My decade long struggle had allowed me to travel far and learn much. I share my story in the hopes of helping you with yours.

My mother's question is simple, but the answer isn't easy. I've thought about the things I hadn't adequately given enough attention to in order to navigate my way through my career expansion and I've come up with some thoughts that help me as I keep on traveling.

Know Who You Are and Where You Are

I felt as I launched out to pursue my dreams that I had a pretty good idea as to my sense of identity. I'm a sort of take charge person that desires to be in control. I also like to know as much as possible about what I'm doing and its correlation to my likelihood of success. In hindsight, I've discovered that there were considerable gaps in my knowledge base. My strengths didn't offset my weaknesses. Because I like control, I pay a lot of attention to detail. My problem was that I made little preparation for circumstances that were beyond my control.

I knew me, but I didn't know fully where I was when I launched out on my own. I didn't have funds set aside to meet my needs should things go wrong. Not only had I not built a financial margin to fall back on, I was in debt. I had obligations that required my attention. You may think that those are basic considerations for someone about to quit their job and go on a life changing journey and you'd be right. I was so confident as a result of early successes that reality hadn't managed to make enough of an impression.

Knowing yourself is crucial to making a career change. I thought I understood myself, but I discovered the downside of my personality too late to be of benefit. Wanting to be in control but then losing control was hard to withstand. I hadn't given any thought to that. Two questions I should have asked myself were: How will you hold up under stress? and: Do you have enough living and working capital to make a go of it? These are two questions I would have done well to have considered. I had nothing saved for the lean times, nor was I prepared for the emotional and physical strains and stresses that came in waves.

I'm now more measured in my efforts, having come to realize

how easily things can shift. I'm diligently working toward my dreams but I'm also working to position myself to withstand future lean times. This gives me a better sense of control, allowing me to remain creative so that I'm better able to accomplish my goals.

Know How to Read a Map

I should have taken the time to write out a business plan. Every trip over long distances involves a map. Making a career transition, or in my case, a career expansion, requires careful planning. Writing down the plan makes it possible to scrutinize; it makes the journey more real when you can see it on paper. I failed to do that.

By writing out a life plan or business plan you're better able to ascertain direction, and direction equals decision. If I had just put forth more effort and developed a written plan to chart the course, I would have derived the direction I needed to go in and that would have impacted my decisions. Seeing finances laid out on paper, writing a list of pros and cons regarding an idea, putting a checklist together that maps out the first, second and third steps—these would have been of great benefit in my decision making process.

There is just something about creating a map and then following the map that gives a clear perspective. I was blinded by the speed and distance I was enjoying, to such extent that I missed many road signs that contained messages I really couldn't afford missing. Sometimes when you get lost it's better to pull off to the side of the road and read the map.

Know When to Change Course

I learned this lesson when I began to be pressured by unrelenting financial pain. I still hope for, and am working toward, financial independence. I have a hope and a plan to serve in ministry in the future without any consideration of income. If I feel led to work in ministry with a congregation that can't pay a salary, no problem; money won't have to become a determining factor. But that day is not yet. I had to make a course correction or I would have lost hope of ever being in a position to carry out the dream birthed in me.

We each must learn to smell the coffee. We must be alert early when things begin to go wrong. Wake-up calls will come like those metallic ridges built in roads along the lanes of highways that make a noise when we drift over the lines. I saw that I was making no progress after leaving my interim position, but I waited longer than I should have in securing full-time employment. I knew after I had made the first course correction that I needed to be prepared to make others.

This is not an easy thing to accept because it feels as though you've failed. I felt that way, but I came to realize that failing doesn't make a person a failure; quitting makes us failures. Giving up and interpreting setbacks as a sign to quit is naive and foolish. Anything worthwhile will have inherent trouble. I fully intend to one day, after many years of struggle through blood, sweat and tears, become an overnight sensation!

Know the Joy of Getting There

I can't spend time in my life rehashing the bad decisions, the mistakes, or the ensuing pain that resulted. It would be a fruitless waste of time and energy to hover over the past. Instead, I've come to see that there is a certain joy in the process of traveling along on my career expansion journey. Don't get me wrong, I still sting from the bumps and bruises suffered along the way. But I now know more than I did then, and I have incorporated that new knowledge into my map so that I can travel farther by being better prepared.

I've always been focused, sometimes too much so. I would often get so absorbed with goals that I failed to derive any enjoyment in the journey. I was so busy *doing* that I neglected *being*—being with family and being content in present blessings. Just being. After all, life is more than success and achievement. It's about living and making the most of your presence among those you love. It's also about serving God by serving others.

I can still hear my mother saying, "Do you know where you are now?" Yes, mom, I do. I'm still on the road and I'm still figuring things out, but I'm getting there. I'm content to live each day in such a way as to make a lasting difference. At the risk of grammar violation: I want to be the me God created me to be. I reckon that will take a lifetime to accomplish.

A Closing Thought From Ben and Ken

There is a famous Japanese proverb that reflects Lou's tenacity: "Fall seven times, stand up eight." Lou is the perfect example of why some people seem to always succeed—they just refuse to give up.

All successful people establish high goals then set out to reach them. Many discover, despite planning and good intentions, that some dreams are unrealized. Lou discovered this unfortunate truth, but refused to let it kill his aspiration of financial independence. He's continued to get up every time there has been a challenge.

No dream is ever realized without some setbacks. The secret to Lou's ultimate success is his indomitable spirit and focus of never taking his eye off the ultimate goal.

This may well be the secret you've been searching for in your bonus years. When life seems to dash your dreams, don't let it be the ultimate victor. No matter how many times you fall, get up one more time.

Chapter 12

ARE YOU READY FOR YOUR OVERTIME BONUS YEARS?

Ben Dickerson and Ken Arthur

You have now read stories written by creative and determined individuals. At some point in each story, hopefully you've recognized yourself—either where you are right now or where you would like to be. These authors have all made distinct decisions that made their bonus years meaningful.

Don't be concerned if your personal story isn't even remotely the same as anyone you've read about here. The unique expression you give to life's events are what will make your story special.

You have no reason to judge your experiences by anyone else's standards. After all, you don't have the same combination of talents, gifts, and abilities as anyone else, but they don't have yours either. We are all given uniqueness by the Creator.

So then, as a unique individual, are you ready for your bonus years? Learn from others. Take their experiences and make them tools to craft your life.

What you can do with your unique combination of talents, gifts, and abilities largely depends on your openness and willingness to do what these authors have done. They've refused to be stuck in the past or even in the present, they've taken calculated risks, they've been willing to face their fears and move on, and they've dreamed big dreams.

How do you do that in your overtime years? First, you have to *suit up* to get in the game.

No professional football player would ever get on the field to play any game unless they were suited up in their personal equipment. Notice the next time you watch a football game on TV that each player has specialized equipment for their position. The equipment does more than protect the player; it also enhances his effectiveness. For example, the quarterback's shoulder pads are less cumbersome than a 300 pound lineman's shoulder pads. Each player is required to wear a helmet, but there are different face masks depending upon the position. Linemen, whose role involves grappling with other huge men throughout an entire game, have many bars that protect their eyes but somewhat limit their vision. Receivers, who must see the ball clearly and don't get hands in their faces, have fewer bars in their face masks, which allow for greater visibility. Kickers, who are protected by the rules from receiving hits, usually have a single face mask bar, allowing them the best possible vision.

The equipment a football team brings to their game changes when they encounter different situations. For example, they use one kind of shoe for playing on artificial turf, and entirely different shoes for playing on natural turf. Flexibility in the use of specialized equipment and the willingness to adapt are crucial to the team's success.

Likewise, for you to reach fullness in your bonus years, you have to cultivate and integrate some specialized *equipment,* or characteristics, into your life.

Perhaps some of the authors you met in this book showed characteristics with which you identified or have longed to develop in your life. While each author is unique, they have all shown some similar characteristics. For purposes of our football analogy, these characteristics are their *equipment.*

The authors of this chapter believe for you to grow or progress in your bonus years, you need to suit up with some absolutely crucial equipment such as:

• Attitude – Attitude precedes behavior. It includes believing in yourself. It determines your perspective. Is the glass half full or half empty? It's confidence, not arrogance. Attitude is the key that unlocks the bonus years.

• Core Values – Core values are what you consider to be of the highest worth or importance. They significantly influence the way you will behave in certain circumstances. For example, students who want to excel in school might sacrifice a social life, sleep, or even eating in order to study and make the highest possible scores on an exam. To these students, high scores are central to their core values and influence their behavior. To put it another way, core values are like a compass that gives you direction in your pursuit of life satisfaction. Assess your core values, determine what gives your life direction, and decide what goals and behaviors will always be important to you.

• Courage to Leave Your Comfort Zone – To reach the goals we set for ourselves in the bonus years, often we have to be willing to try something new. This takes courage and belief in yourself. For example, some people would rather be miserable in a dead-end job than to dust off their résumé and risk starting over with a new company. It does take courage to face change, but that courage can be rewarded by renewed challenges, fulfillment, and fun. This kind of courage involves more than just your job. It means changing or altering anything that is merely comfortable but does not bring you satisfaction in return.

• Persistence – There is absolutely no substitute for persistence. You will always have someone or something to stand in the way of your dreams. Resisting the urge to quit or continuing in the face of criticism is necessary for reaching any goal. However, don't let hard headedness or stubbornness masquerade as persistence. If you discover that your path is no longer appropriate or fulfilling, be willing to change directions or even start over. Also, recognize that persistence can become an obsession. A horse with blinders on will continue in a straight line because it can't see any options for other directions. Likewise, this happens when a person unwaveringly continues along a straight path but the route to the destination has changed. Persistence works when you know your direction and objective are valid.

• Patience – Have patience with yourself, others and situations. Patience with others can be the easiest to develop. Simply acknowledging that someone is doing his or her best can be enough to evoke patience. The biblical scripture found in Matthew 7:5 helps, too. It reminds us to take care of the things in our own lives before trying to look for faults in others. Events always work in their own timeframe. You sometimes have control over schedules and situations, but more often, very little control. An impatient person is extremely susceptible to the most insidious danger—stress. The bonus years are uncharted territory. Being patient with yourself while navigating these years is a way of lessening that stress. You're learning new skills, taking new risks, and discovering new pathways. There are bound to be missteps. Don't be too hard on yourself as you explore the new terrain called the bonus years. Again, be patient with yourself, with others and with situations.

• Vision – Vision is the ability to see opportunities that others miss or simply may not recognize. Vision means trusting your intuition or insight in recognizing new possibilities to be a trailblazer or pioneer. If you don't perceive it, you can't use it to reach your goals.

• Energy – Many people allow their physical health to slide as they grow older. This may rob their bonus years of the physical energy they need. Seeing your physician regularly and following his or her advice regarding appropriate exercise programs and nutrition are crucial to maintaining your energy level. Maintaining your mental energy is equally crucial. For example, to tone your mind, read a wide variety of books, find intellectually challenging games and puzzles, look for hobbies and interests beyond what you've always done. By exercising your brain, you help keep your mental energy sharp. These cerebral exercises also help you avoid boredom, which may lead to depression or apathy.

• Toughness – Toughness goes hand-in-hand with persistence. You have to stick to your plans regardless of obstacles that come in your path. There will always be those who find it easier to criticize or second guess you than to support you. You have to develop the mental toughness it takes to withstand the sarcasm of comments such as, You're going to do WHAT? You've GOT to be kidding! Stay the course when you know you're right. A second benefit of a good exercise and nutrition program, beyond energy, is physical toughness. As you mature, it's easy to allow your body to atrophy from neglect. Remember, to fully enjoy *your bonus years*, you have to possess the physical stamina to embrace them.

• Passion – Passion is a magnificent word. Passion connotes a fervent love affair, an all encompassing desire for someone or something. Passion is such a strong emotion, and that's what we are encouraging for you. Having a passion for squeezing every drop of life from your bonus years is a gift you give yourself. Losing yourself in some exciting new adventure keeps the passion of life fresh. Passion makes time meaningless. When you're with someone you adore, time doesn't matter. You enjoy every second, every breath, every sunset even more. Having a passion for what you're doing brings a luster to your bonus years that makes every moment indescribable.

• Honesty With Yourself – We've all heard, "If you put your mind to something, you can accomplish anything." That sounds good, but at some point in life, it's not really true. If you're in your bonus years, chances are this isn't a good time to begin training to be an Olympic gymnast or a professional soccer player. That's not realistic. Setting honest goals and having down-to-earth ambitions involves being honest with yourself. Is it too late to begin a master's or doctoral degree? Probably not. Is it beyond reason to sail across the Atlantic? With proper training and equipment, no, it is not. Is it still an option to climb Mount Everest? Don't know why you would want to, but it's possibly still attainable. Make your plans with a basic honesty with yourself. You'll be amazed at what possibilities still exist for you to stretch yourself in the bonus years.

• Adaptation – We face modification every day of our lives, but as we said earlier, many people don't adapt well to change. They're comfortable doing what they've always done and prefer a routine that involves little variation. However, life requires adaptation, and this realization is sometimes difficult for us. Have you ever heard the comment, "Life has passed me by"? Life will not pass anyone who is looking for the detours and making the turns as they come. Be willing to make alterations to your plans when something new develops. Recognize the fact that nothing will *ever* go exactly as planned. Be flexible enough to change with them.

• Sense of Humor – An antidote for being too serious. Nothing eases friction in any situation better than humor. Everyone appreciates a person who can laugh at himself and at awkward circumstances. Nothing can take the sting out of a painful event like the balm of a liberal dose of humor. Often in our bonus years we find more time to watch television. Some people we know spend those extra hours watching the shows that emphasize the seedier side of life ... and you know what we mean. How much happier would they be and how much more positive would their outlook be if instead they watched old reruns of *I Love Lucy* or *Andy Griffith* or any of those classic shows we still laugh at regardless of the number of times we've seen them? Many of the classic comic strips have been compiled and bound into books. Buy one for each bathroom. Basically, find any excuse or opportunity to laugh and develop your sense of humor.

All of these characteristics are important, but only a positive attitude is absolutely essential in every situation. During any given day, you will need to call upon different resources depending upon the circumstances you face. For example, in the morning, a sense of humor might be the most useful tool to manage a specific event, but later the same day you might need to show toughness to manage a different situation. Again, flexibility and judgment are learned abilities. Practice thinking before acting.

Don't look back. The first four quarters have ended. Overtime is a completely new beginning. Every coach in the NFL teaches his players that once they catch a ball, they should never look back. Instead they are taught to keep their eyes ahead to the goal line. In the same way, don't limit yourself to your life up to this point. It's over and done with. Keep looking ahead. Ralph Waldo Emerson said it best:

Finish every day and be done with it. You have done what you could. Some blunders and absurdities no doubt crept in; forget them as soon as you can. Tomorrow is a new day; begin it well and serenely, and with too high a spirit to be cumbered with your old nonsense. This day is all that is good and fair. It is too dear, with its hopes and invitations, to waste a moment on the yesterdays.

The Game Clock Has Been Reset

Your overtime is beginning. The coin is in the air. Call it ... heads or tails. What are you going to do with this new beginning in your overtime? Enjoy the overtime bonus years and win big!

Bibliography

Buford, Bob. 2004. *Finishing Well: What People Who Really Live Do Differently!* Nashville, TN: Integrity Publishers.

---. 1997. *Game Plan: Winning Strategies for the Second Half of Your Life.* Grand Rapids, MI: Zondervan Publishing House.

---. 1994. *Half Time: Changing Your Game Plan From Success to Significance.* Grand Rapids, MI: Zondervan Publishing House.

Cohen, Gene, M.D., Ph.D. 2000. *The Creative Age: Awakening Human Potential in the Second Half of Life.* New York: HarperCollins Publishers.

Cooper, Kenneth, M.D. 1998. *Regaining the Power of Youth at Any Age: Startling New Evidence From the Doctor Who Brought Us Aerobics, Controlling Cholesterol and the Antioxidant Revolution, Part One.* Nashville, TN: Thomas Nelson, Inc.

Eldredge, John. 2001. *Wild at Heart: Discovering the Secret of a Man's Soul.* Nashville: Thomas Nelson, Inc.

Freedman, Marc. 1999. *Prime Time: How Baby Boomers Will Revolutionize Retirement and Transform America.* 24. New York: Perseus Books.

Groeschel, Craig. 2006. *Chazown: "khaw-ZONE" – A Different Way to See Your Life.* Sisters, OR: Multnomah Publishers.

Hindery, Leo Jr. and Leslie Cauley. 2003. *The Biggest Game of All: The Inside Strategies, Tactics, and Temperaments That Make Great Dealmakers Great.* New York: Free Press.

LeFevre, Mylon. 2003. *How Blessed Do You Want to Be?: Make the Choice That Makes the Difference.* Tulsa: Harrison House.

Lorayne, Harry and Jerry Lucas. 1975. *The Memory Book: The Classic Guide to Improving Your Memory at Work, at School, and at Play.* New York: Ballantine Publishing Group.

Lucado, Max. 2001. *Traveling Light: Releasing the Burdens You Were Never Intended to Bear.* Nashville: W Publishing Group.

Maxwell, John C. 2004. *Today Matters: 12 Daily Practices to Guarantee Tomorrow's Success.* New York: Warner Faith Publishing, a Time Warner Book Group.

McCormack, Mark H. 1986. *What They Don't Teach You at Harvard Business School: Notes from a Street-Smart Executive.* New York: Bantam Books.

McVeigh, Kate. 2003. *The Blessings of Favor: Experiencing God's Supernatural Influence.* Tulsa: Harrison House.

Popcorn, Faith and Lys Marigold. 1996. *Clicking: 16 Trends to Future Fit Your Life, Your Work, and Your Business.* New York: HarperCollins Publishers.

Townsend, Robert. 1970. *Up the Organization: How to Stop the Corporation From Stifling People and Strangling Profits.* New York: Alfred A. Knopf, Inc.

---. 1984. *Further Up the Organization: How Groups of People Working Together for a Common Purpose Ought to Conduct Themselves for Fun and Profit.* New York: Alfred A. Knopf, Inc.

Zelinski, Ernie J. 2003. *The Joy of Not Working: A Book for the Retired, Unemployed, and Overworked.* Berkeley: Ten Speed Press.

Ziglar, Zig. 2006. *Better Than Good: Creating a Life You Can't Wait to Live.* Nashville, TN: Integrity Publishers.

Printed in the United States
73778LV00001B/199-999